THE NEW "PANORAMA" BIBLE STUDY COURSE No. 4

"A VISUAL STUDY OF THE BOOK OF REVELATION"

ALFRED THOMPSON EADE S.T.D.

Copyright © 1970 by Fleming H. Revell
a division of Baker Book House Company
P.O. Box 6287, Grand Rapids, MI 49516-6287
All rights reserved

ISBN: 0-8007-0434-7

Printed in the United States of America

For current information about all releases from Baker Book House, visit our web site:
http://www.bakerbooks.com

The "Panorama" Bible Study Charts, and reproductions of the same, are fully protected by copyright, and may not be reproduced in any form without the written permission of the publisher or author.

Fleming H. Revell
A Division of Baker Book House
Grand Rapids, Michigan 49506

STUDY 1 — "THE THINGS WHICH THOU HAST SEEN," CHAPTER 1

— THE VISION OF THE GLORIFIED CHRIST —

"IN THE MIDST OF THE SEVEN CANDLESTICKS ONE LIKE UNTO THE SON OF MAN...HE HAD IN HIS RIGHT HAND SEVEN STARS ...I FELL AT HIS FEET AS DEAD -- THE SEVEN STARS ARE THE SEVEN ANGELS [MESSENGERS] OF THE SEVEN CHURCHES...THE SEVEN CANDLESTICKS ARE THE SEVEN CHURCHES." CHAP 1:12-18.

EPHESUS SMYRNA PERGAMOS THYATIRA SARDIS PHILADELPHIA LAODICEA

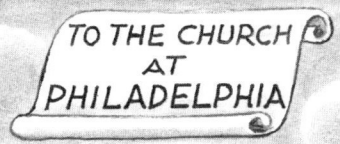

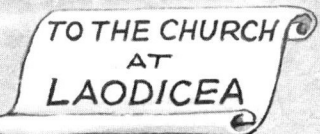

STUDY 2 — "THE THINGS WHICH ARE" — CHAPTERS 2 AND 3

REFERRING PRIMARILY TO THE SEVEN CHURCHES, BUT, UNMISTAKABLY A PROPHETIC FOREVIEW OF THE SUCCESSIVE PERIODS OF CHURCH HISTORY — FROM THE APOSTOLIC DAYS TO THE END OF THIS PRESENT AGE ("THE CHURCH AGE" ~ "THE AGE OF GRACE" — FROM PENTECOST TO THE RAPTURE)

PENTECOST — THE RAPTURE

"...CHURCH OF THE FIRSTBORN, WHICH ARE WRITTEN IN HEAVEN..." HEB. 12:22

TO THE CHURCH AT EPHESUS	TO THE CHURCH AT SMYRNA	TO THE CHURCH AT PERGAMOS	TO THE CHURCH AT THYATIRA	TO THE CHURCH AT SARDIS	TO THE CHURCH AT PHILADELPHIA	TO THE CHURCH AT LAODICEA
REV. 2:1-7	REV. 2:8-11	REV. 2:12-17	REV. 2:18-29	REV. 3:1-6	REV. 3:7-13	REV. 3:14-22

EPHESUS
Means "Desirable"
THE CHURCH AS IT WAS IN THE APOSTOLIC BEGINNING ** WHEN THE LORD HELD THE "STARS" (HIS MINISTERS) IN HIS RIGHT HAND. THE PLACE OF POSSESSION AND AUTHORITY. HE WAS IN THEIR MIDST. THUS THE CHURCH WALKED IN SEPARATION FROM THE WORLD. THIS WAS GOD'S "DESIRABLE" • HE REPROVED THEM, HOWEVER, FOR LEAVING THEIR FIRST LOVE.

SMYRNA
Means "myrrh" (actually bitter) USED IN THE HOLY INCENSE, TO BE CRUSHED TO GIVE FORTH IT'S FRAGRANCE. FIERCE PERSECUTION HAD IT'S CENTER IN SMYRNA. THE ASSEMBLY WAS CRUSHED UNDER THE STRINGENT IMPERIAL LAWS AGAINST CHRISTIANITY; YET THE FRAGRANCE OF THEIR DEVOTION TRIUMPHED ABOVE THE TWO CENTURIES UNDER THE EMPERORS OF PAGAN ROME.

PERGAMOS
Meaning "a mixed marriage" & "elevation" BEGINNING WITH THE CONVERSION OF CONSTANTINE WHO DECLARED CHRISTIANITY, ONCE CONDEMNED AS HERESY AGAINST THE STATE, NOW TO BE THE STATE RELIGION. BY HIS FAVOR PERSECUTION CEASED AND THE CLERGY EXALTED BY THE ALLIANCE WITH THE WORLD, WHERE, THE LETTER DECLARED, "SATAN'S SEAT (THRONE) IS"

THYATIRA
IN PRESENTING HIMSELF TO THIS ASSEMBLY AS "THE SON OF GOD" FORESEEING THE RAPID RISE OF ROMANISM, OUR LORD WOULD HAVE SUCCESSIVE GENERATIONS KNOW THAT HE ALONE IS SUPREME IN THE FINAL AUTHORITY. THAT IN HIS FOREKNOWLEDGE THE SAD CONDITION OF THE CHURCH AT THYATIRA WAS PROPHETIC OF THAT PERIOD OF CHURCH HISTORY TO BE RECORDED AS "THE DARK AGES."

SARDIS
THE NAME SARDIS, TO THE CHURCH, IMPLIES "ESCAPING ONES" — "THOSE WHO COME OUT." THOUGH THE CHURCH WAS CONSIDERED SPIRITUAL FROM EXTERNAL OBSERVATION, BY ALL SPIRITUAL STANDARDS IT WAS DEAD. IN THE MIDST OF SPIRITUAL DECEPTION THERE WAS A REMNANT OF WORTHY ONES, AS THE NAME IMPLIES. THIS DESCRIPTION IS SEEN TO CULMINATE IN HISTORY, AS THE GREAT REFORMATION.

PHILADELPHIA
Means "Brotherly love"
CHRIST DECLARED "I HAVE SET BEFORE THEE AN OPEN DOOR." THE FAITHFUL TESTIMONY OF THE ASSEMBLY WAS MADE POSSIBLE BY CHRIST KEEPING OPEN THE DOOR AGAINST ALL OPPOSING FORCES. THIS ASSURANCE MAY BE TRULY PROPHETIC OF THE ERA OF WORLD-WIDE EVANGELISM WHICH FOLLOWED "THE GREAT REFORMATION."

LAODICEA
MEANS THE RULE OR WILL OF THE PEOPLE. CHRIST ADDRESSES HIMSELF AS THE "AMEN." CONFIRMING ALL THAT HE HAD COMMANDED JOHN TO WRITE. FINDING NOTHING BUT SELF-SATISFACTION AND MATERIAL RICHES, OUR LORD REMINDS THEM OF THEIR SPIRITUAL POVERTY, AND HIS DISAPPOINTMENT, WITH THE FORCEFUL WORDS " BECAUSE THOU ART LUKEWARM I WILL SPUE THEE OUT OF MY MOUTH."

APOSTOLIC — A.D. 160 — A.D. 313 — THE DARK AGES — A.D. 1517 — A.D. 1750 — THE LAST DAYS

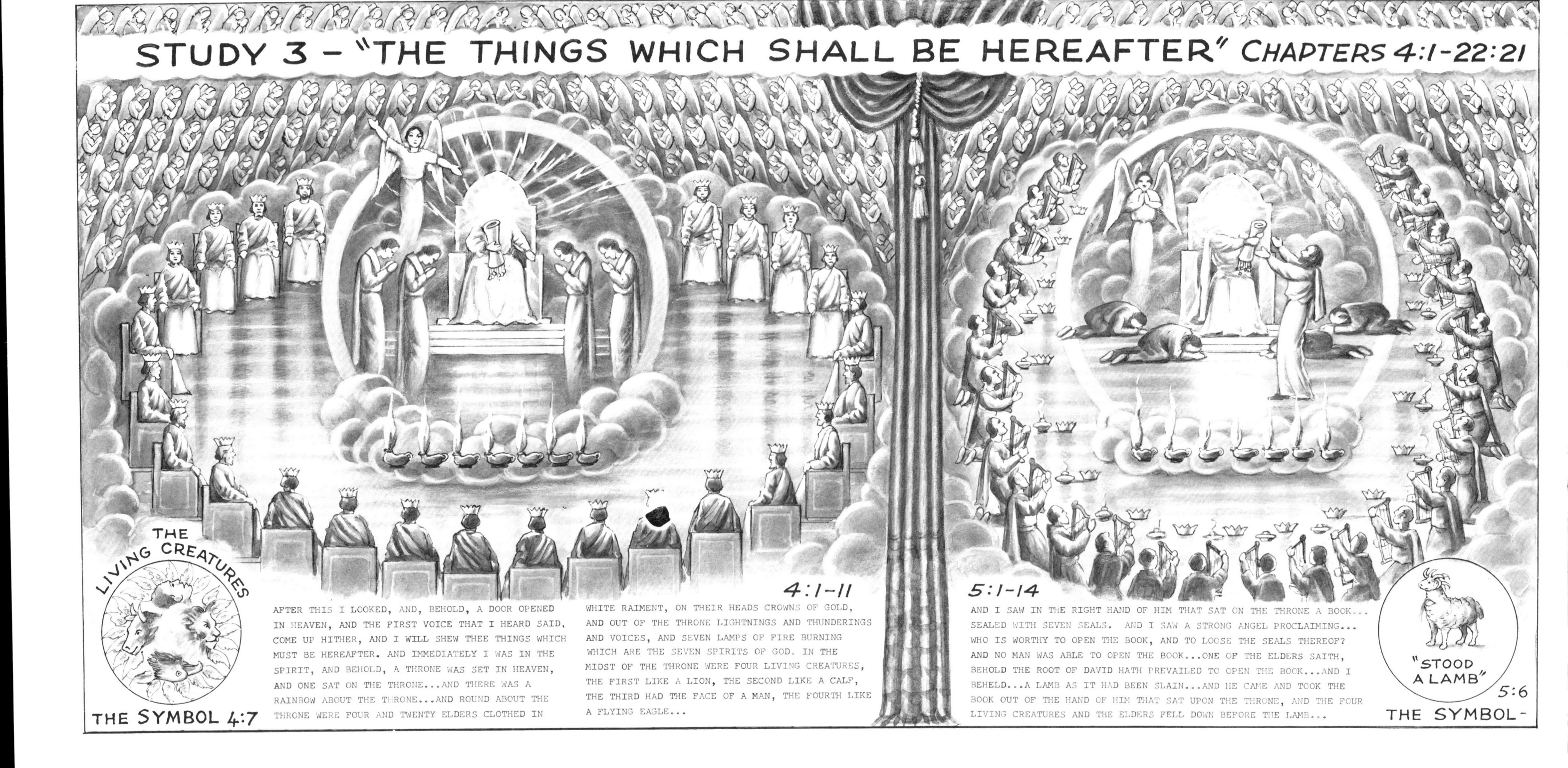

STUDY 3 – "THE THINGS WHICH SHALL BE HEREAFTER" CHAPTERS 4:1-22:21

THE LIVING CREATURES

THE SYMBOL 4:7

4:1-11

AFTER THIS I LOOKED, AND, BEHOLD, A DOOR OPENED IN HEAVEN, AND THE FIRST VOICE THAT I HEARD SAID, COME UP HITHER, AND I WILL SHEW THEE THINGS WHICH MUST BE HEREAFTER. AND IMMEDIATELY I WAS IN THE SPIRIT, AND BEHOLD, A THRONE WAS SET IN HEAVEN, AND ONE SAT ON THE THRONE...AND THERE WAS A RAINBOW ABOUT THE THRONE...AND ROUND ABOUT THE THRONE WERE FOUR AND TWENTY ELDERS CLOTHED IN WHITE RAIMENT, ON THEIR HEADS CROWNS OF GOLD, AND OUT OF THE THRONE LIGHTNINGS AND THUNDERINGS AND VOICES, AND SEVEN LAMPS OF FIRE BURNING WHICH ARE THE SEVEN SPIRITS OF GOD. IN THE MIDST OF THE THRONE WERE FOUR LIVING CREATURES, THE FIRST LIKE A LION, THE SECOND LIKE A CALF, THE THIRD HAD THE FACE OF A MAN, THE FOURTH LIKE A FLYING EAGLE...

5:1-14

AND I SAW IN THE RIGHT HAND OF HIM THAT SAT ON THE THRONE A BOOK... SEALED WITH SEVEN SEALS. AND I SAW A STRONG ANGEL PROCLAIMING... WHO IS WORTHY TO OPEN THE BOOK, AND TO LOOSE THE SEALS THEREOF? AND NO MAN WAS ABLE TO OPEN THE BOOK...ONE OF THE ELDERS SAITH, BEHOLD THE ROOT OF DAVID HATH PREVAILED TO OPEN THE BOOK...AND I BEHELD...A LAMB AS IT HAD BEEN SLAIN...AND HE CAME AND TOOK THE BOOK OUT OF THE HAND OF HIM THAT SAT UPON THE THRONE, AND THE FOUR LIVING CREATURES AND THE ELDERS FELL DOWN BEFORE THE LAMB...

"STOOD A LAMB" 5:6

THE SYMBOL-

STUDY 3 (CONTINUED) "THE THINGS WHICH SHALL BE HEREAFTER"

"WORTHY IS THE LAMB TO OPEN THE BOOK AND TO LOOSEN THE SEALS"

1ST SEAL CONQUEST	2ND SEAL WAR	3RD SEAL FAMINE	4TH SEAL DEATH

THE FOUR HORSEMEN OF THE APOCALYPSE

A WHITE HORSE 6:2

AND I SAW WHEN THE LAMB OPENED ONE OF THE SEALS, AND I HEARD, AS IT WERE THE NOISE OF THUNDER, ONE OF THE FOUR LIVING CREATURES SAYING, COME AND SEE. AND I SAW, AND BEHOLD A WHITE HORSE: AND HE THAT SAT ON HIM HAD A BOW; AND A CROWN WAS GIVEN UNTO HIM: AND HE WENT FORTH CONQUERING, AND TO CONQUER.

A RED HORSE 6:4

WHEN HE HAD OPENED THE SECOND SEAL, I HEARD THE SECOND LIVING CREATURE SAY, COME AND SEE. AND THERE WENT OUT ANOTHER HORSE THAT WAS RED: AND POWER WAS GIVEN TO HIM THAT SAT THEREON TO TAKE PEACE FROM THE EARTH, AND THAT THEY SHOULD KILL ONE ANOTHER: AND THERE WAS GIVEN HIM A GREAT SWORD.

A BLACK HORSE 6:5

AND WHEN HE HAD OPENED THE THIRD SEAL, I HEARD THE THIRD LIVING CREATURE SAY, COME AND SEE. AND I BEHELD, AND LO A BLACK HORSE; AND HE THAT SAT ON HIM HAD A PAIR OF BALANCES IN HIS HAND. AND I HEARD A VOICE SAY, A MEASURE OF WHEAT FOR A PENNY, AND THREE MEASURES OF BARLEY FOR A PENNY; AND SEE THOU HURT NOT THE OIL AND THE WINE.

A PALE HORSE 6:8

AND WHEN HE HAD OPENED THE FOURTH SEAL...I LOOKED, AND BEHOLD A PALE HORSE: AND HIS NAME THAT SAT ON HIM WAS DEATH, AND HELL FOLLOWED WITH HIM. AND POWER WAS GIVEN UNTO THEM OVER THE FOURTH PART OF THE EARTH, TO KILL WITH SWORD, AND WITH HUNGER, AND WITH DEATH AND WITH THE BEASTS OF THE EARTH.

5TH SEAL MARTYRED SOULS IN HEAVEN

6:9-11

TRIBULATION SAINTS SLAIN FOR THE WORD OF GOD AND THEIR TESTIMONY

WHEN HE HAD OPENED THE FIFTH SEAL, I SAW UNDER THE ALTAR THE SOULS OF THEM THAT WERE SLAIN FOR THE WORD OF GOD, AND FOR THE TESTIMONY THAT THEY HELD. AND THEY CRIED WITH A LOUD VOICE, SAYING, HOW LONG, O LORD, DOST THOU NOT JUDGE AND AVENGE OUR BLOOD ON THEM THAT DWELL ON THE EARTH. AND WHITE ROBES WERE GIVEN UNTO EVERY ONE OF THEM; AND IT WAS SAID UNTO THEM, THA' THEY SHOULD REST FOR A LITTLE SEASON; UNTIL THEIR FELLOW-SERVANTS...THAT SHOULD BE KILLED AS THEY WERE, BE FULFILLED.

STUDY 3 (CONTINUED) — "THE THINGS WHICH SHALL BE HEREAFTER" — THE SEALS RESUMED

CHAP. 7 - INTERLUDE BETWEEN SEALS

6TH SEAL
6:12-17

6:12-17

UNDER THE 6TH SEAL GOD BEGINS TO DEAL JUDICIALLY WITH THE WORLD— "THE GREAT DAY OF HIS WRATH IS COME"

I BEHELD WHEN HE HAD OPENED THE SIXTH SEAL THERE WAS A GREAT EARTHQUAKE; AND THE SUN BECAME BLACK AS SACKCLOTH OF HAIR, AND THE MOON BECAME AS BLOOD; AND THE STARS OF THE HEAVENS FELL INTO THE EARTH...AND [ALL MEN] HID THEMSELVES IN THE DENS AND IN THE ROCKS OF THE MOUNTAINS; AND SAID, FALL ON US, AND HIDE US FROM THE FACE OF HIM THAT SITTETH ON THE THRONE, AND FROM THE WRATH OF THE LAMB: FOR THE GREAT DAY OF HIS WRATH IS COME: AND WHO SHALL BE ABLE TO STAND?

SIMEON
REUBEN
JUDA
ASER
ZABULON
MANASSES
GAD
JOSEPH
NEPHALIM
ISSACHAR
BENJAMIN
LEVI

7:1-8

THE 144,000 - 12 THOUSAND FROM EACH TRIBE OF ISRAEL SEALED BY "THE SEAL OF THE LIVING GOD"

AFTER THESE THINGS I SAW FOUR ANGELS...HOLDING THE FOUR WINDS OF THE EARTH...AND I SAW ANOTHER ANGEL FROM THE EAST, HAVING THE SEAL OF THE LIVING GOD: AND HE CRIED WITH A LOUD VOICE TO THE FOUR ANGELS...SAYING, HURT NOT...TILL WE HAVE SEALED THE SERVANTS OF OUR GOD IN THEIR FOREHEADS. AND I HEARD THE NUMBER OF THEM WHICH WERE SEALED: AND THERE WERE SEALED AN HUNDRED AND FORTY AND FOUR THOUSAND OF ALL THE TRIBES OF THE CHILDREN OF ISRAEL...

7:9-17

THE WHITE ROBED PALM-BEARING MULTITUDE · "THESE ARE THEY WHICH CAME OUT OF TRIBULATION"

AFTER THIS I BEHELD, AND LO, A GREAT MULTITUDE, WHICH NO MAN COULD NUMBER...STOOD BEFORE THE THRONE, AND BEFORE THE LAMB, CLOTHED WITH WHITE ROBES, AND PALMS IN THEIR HANDS; AND CRIED WITH A LOUD VOICE, SAYING, SALVATION TO OUR GOD WHICH SITTETH UPON THE THRONE, AND TO THE LAMB...ONE OF THE ELDERS ANSWERED, SAYING UNTO ME, THESE ARE THEY WHICH CAME OUT OF GREAT TRIBULATION, AND HAVE WASHED THEIR ROBES AND MADE THEM WHITE IN THE BLOOD OF THE LAMB.

7TH SEAL

8:1-6

THE SEVEN TRUMPET ANGELS OF GOD'S PRESENCE · EACH TO SOUND A BLAST OF ONCOMING JUDGMENT

WHEN HE HAD OPENED THE SEVENTH SEAL...I SAW THE SEVEN ANGELS WHICH STOOD BEFORE GOD; AND TO THEM WAS GIVEN SEVEN TRUMPETS. AND ANOTHER ANGEL CAME AND STOOD AT THE ALTAR, HAVING A GOLDEN CENSER: AND THERE WAS GIVEN UNTO HIM MUCH INCENSE, THAT HE SHOULD OFFER IT WITH THE PRAYERS OF ALL SAINTS UPON THE GOLDEN ALTAR...AND THE ANGEL TOOK THE CENSER, AND FILLED IT WITH FIRE OF THE ALTAR, AND CAST IT INTO THE EARTH: AND THERE WERE THUNDERINGS, AND LIGHTNINGS, AND AN EARTHQUAKE.

STUDY 3 (CONTINUED) "THE THINGS WHICH SHALL BE HEREAFTER"

THE TRUMPET JUDGMENTS

THE FIRST TRUMPET

ONE THIRD PART OF ALL VEGETATION DESTROYED BY FIRE AND HAIL · 8:7

THE TRUMPET JUDGMENTS
***
AND THE SEVEN ANGELS WHICH HAD THE SEVEN TRUMPETS PREPARED THEMSELVES TO SOUND. THE FIRST ANGEL SOUNDED AND THERE FOLLOWED HAIL AND FIRE MINGLED WITH BLOOD, AND THE THIRD PART OF TREES WAS BURNT UP, AND ALL GREEN GRASS WAS BURNT UP.

THE SECOND TRUMPET

8:8-9
ONE THIRD PART SEA BECOMES BLOOD · ONE THIRD LIFE DESTROYED

AND THE SECOND ANGEL SOUNDED, AND AS IT WERE A GREAT MOUNTAIN BURNING WITH FIRE WAS CAST INTO THE SEA: AND THE THIRD PART OF THE SEA BECAME BLOOD; AND THE THIRD PART OF THE CREATURES WHICH WERE IN THE SEA, AND HAD LIFE, DIED, AND THE THIRD PART OF THE SHIPS WERE DESTROYED.

THE THIRD TRUMPET

A FALLING STAR EMBITTERS ONE THIRD OF THE RIVERS AND FOUNTAINS – 8:10-11

AND THE THIRD ANGEL SOUNDED, AND THERE FELL A GREAT STAR FROM HEAVEN, BURNING AS IT WERE A LAMP, AND IT FELL UPON THE THIRD PART OF THE RIVERS, AND UPON THE FOUNTAINS OF WATERS. AND THE NAME OF THE STAR IS CALLED WORMWOOD...AND MANY MEN DIED OF THE WATERS, BECAUSE THEY WERE MADE BITTER.

THE FOURTH TRUMPET

WOE! WOE! WOE!

ONE THIRD PART OF SUN – MOON – STARS DARKENED 8:12-13

AND THE FOURTH ANGEL SOUNDED, AND THE THIRD PART OF THE SUN, THE MOON, AND THE STARS WERE SMITTEN...AND THE DAY SHONE NOT FOR A THIRD PART OF IT, AND THE NIGHT LIKEWISE. AND I BEHELD, AND HEARD AN ANGEL... SAYING, WOE, WOE, WOE TO THE INHABITERS OF THE EARTH...BY REASON OF THE THREE ANGELS YET TO SOUND.

THE FIFTH TRUMPET

THE FIRST WOE!

9:1-12
SATAN LOOSENS DEMONIC TORMENT UPON THE EARTH

AND THE FIFTH ANGEL SOUNDED, AND I SAW A STAR FALL FROM HEAVEN INTO THE EARTH: AND TO HIM WAS GIVEN THE KEY TO THE BOTTOMLESS PIT. AND HE OPENED THE PIT; AND THERE AROSE A SMOKE...AND THERE CAME OUT OF THE SMOKE LOCUSTS UPON THE EARTH...AND MEN SHALL SEEK DEATH AND SHALL NOT FIND IT.

THE SIXTH TRUMPET

LOOSING OF THE FOUR ANGELS AND THE ARMY OF HORSEMEN. 9:13-21

...AND I HEARD A VOICE...SAYING TO THE SIXTH ANGEL WHICH HAD THE TRUMPET, LOOSE THE FOUR ANGELS WHICH ARE BOUND IN THE GREAT RIVER EUPHRATES...WHICH WERE PREPARED TO SLAY THE THIRD PART OF MEN. AND THE NUMBER OF THE HORSEMEN WERE TWO HUNDRED THOUSAND THOUSAND...AND THE HEADS OF THE HORSES WERE AS THE HEADS OF LIONS.

STUDY 3 (CONTINUED) "THE THINGS WHICH SHALL BE HEREAFTER"

← INTERLUDE BETWEEN TRUMPET JUDGMENTS →

← THE TWO WITNESSES →

"NO LONGER DELAY"

11:3-6

"COME UP HITHER"

11:11-12

THE SEVENTH TRUMPET 11:15-19

THE SIGN 12:1-2

ISRAEL

SINAI

"YE SHALL BE UNTO ME... AN HOLY NATION" EX.19:6

THE LORD SHALL GIVE YOU (ISRAEL) A SIGN·A VIRGIN SHALL CONCEIVE AND BEAR A SON AND SHALL CALL HIS NAME IMMANUEL" ISA.7:14

10:1-11
JOHN TO TAKE AND ASSIMILATE THE LITTLE BOOK·THE WORD OF GOD.

AND I SAW ANOTHER MIGHTY ANGEL COME DOWN FROM HEAVEN...AND HE HAD IN HIS HAND A LITTLE BOOK OPEN...AND HE SET HIS RIGHT FOOT UPON THE SEA, AND HIS LEFT FOOT UPON THE EARTH...AND LIFTED UP HIS HAND TO HEAVEN AND SWARE...THAT THERE SHOULD BE DELAY NO LONGER. AND I TOOK THE BOOK AND ATE IT...IN MY MOUTH SWEET AS HONEY AND MY BELLY WAS BITTER...

SLAIN·BUT NOT UNTIL THEIR TESTIMONY IS FINISHED. 11:7-10.

AND I WILL GIVE POWER TO MY TWO WITNESSES AND THEY SHALL PROPHESY A THOUSAND AND TWO HUNDRED AND THREESCORE DAYS...AND WHEN THEY HAVE FINISHED THEIR TESTIMONY THE BEAST SHALL OVERCOME THEM AND KILL THEM. AND THEIR DEAD BODIES SHALL LIE IN THE STREET...AND THEY THAT DWELL UPON THE EARTH SHALL REJOICE OVER THEM...BECAUSE THESE TWO PROPHETS TORMENTED THEM...

THEIR RESURRECTION AND ASCENSION, FOLLOWED BY THE SECOND WOE·11:13-14

AFTER THREE DAYS AND A HALF THE SPIRIT OF LIFE FROM GOD ENTERED INTO THEM AND THEY STOOD UPON THEIR FEET; AND GREAT FEAR FELL UPON THEM WHICH SAW THEM, AND THEY HEARD A GREAT VOICE FROM HEAVEN SAYING, COME UP HITHER. AND THEY ASCENDED UP TO HEAVEN IN A CLOUD AND THEIR ENEMIES BEHELD THEM. AND THE SAME HOUR WAS THERE A GREAT EARTHQUAKE...

SOUNDING OF THE SEVENTH TRUMPET ANNOUNCES THE DOMINION OF THE EARTH IS BECOME CHRIST'S KINGDOM

THE SEVENTH ANGEL SOUNDED; AND THERE WERE GREAT VOICES IN HEAVEN, SAYING, THE KINGDOMS OF THIS WORLD ARE BECOME THE KINGDOM OF OUR LORD, AND OF HIS CHRIST; AND HE SHALL REIGN FOR EVER AND EVER. AND THE FOUR AND TWENTY ELDERS FELL UPON THEIR FACES AND WORSHIPPED GOD...AND THE NATIONS WERE ANGRY...AND THE TEMPLE OF GOD WAS OPEN IN HEAVEN, AND THERE WAS SEEN IN HIS TEMPLE THE ARK OF HIS TESTAMENT. AND THERE WERE LIGHTNINGS AND VOICES, AND THUNDERINGS, AND AN EARTHQUAKE, AND GREAT HAIL...

"UNTIL THE TIME THAT SHE WHICH TRAVAILETH HATH BROUGHT FORTH" MIC 5:3

— THE WOMAN - ISRAEL —
AND THERE APPEARED A GREAT WONDER IN HEAVEN; A WOMAN CLOTHED WITH THE SUN, AND THE MOON UNDER HER FEET, AND UPON HER HEAD A CROWN OF TWELVE STARS: AND SHE BEING WITH CHILD CRIED, TRAVAILING IN BIRTH, AND PAINED TO BE DELIVERED.

STUDY 3 – CONTINUED "THE THINGS WHICH SHALL BE HEREAFTER"

THE SIGN · SATAN 12:3-4

VERSE 9 (CHAP 12) IDENTIFIES THE DRAGON AS SATAN · WITH USURPED AUTHORITY · AS "PRINCE OF THIS WORLD". THE "CASTING DOWN" TRACING HIS CAREER AS "LUCIFER" RECORDED IN ISA. 14:12-15

AND THERE APPEARED ANOTHER WONDER IN HEAVEN; AND BEHOLD A GREAT RED DRAGON, HAVING SEVEN HEADS AND TEN HORNS, AND SEVEN CROWNS UPON HIS HEADS. AND HIS TAIL DREW THE THIRD PART OF THE STARS OF HEAVEN, AND DID CAST THEM TO THE EARTH;

THE MAN CHILD – CHRIST –

"AND SHE BROUGHT FORTH A MAN CHILD" 12:5

THE SLAUGHTER OF THE INNOCENTS – MATT. 2:13-18

"...TO DEVOUR HER CHILD AS SOON AS IT WAS BORN"

AND THE DRAGON STOOD BEFORE THE WOMAN WHICH WAS READY TO BE DELIVERED, FOR TO DEVOUR HER CHILD AS SOON AS IT WAS BORN. (VS. 4) AND SHE BROUGHT FORTH A MAN CHILD, WHO WAS TO RULE ALL NATIONS WITH A ROD OF IRON: (cf. Rev. 19:15-16, Ps. 2, Ps. 72).

CHRIST'S ASCENSION

12:5
"AND HER CHILD WAS CAUGHT UP UNTO GOD AND TO HIS THRONE"

AND WHILE THEY LOOKED STEADFASTLY TOWARD HEAVEN AS HE WENT UP, BEHOLD, TWO MEN STOOD BY THEM IN WHITE APPAREL; WHICH SAID, YE MEN OF GALILEE, WHY STAND YE GAZING UP INTO HEAVEN? THIS SAME JESUS WHICH IS TAKEN UP FROM YOU INTO HEAVEN, SHALL SO COME IN LIKE MANNER AS YE HAVE SEEN HIM GO INTO HEAVEN. Acts 1:10-11

"AND THERE WAS WAR IN HEAVEN" 12:7-12

SATAN - AS "PRINCE OF THE POWER OF THE AIR" CAST OUT OF THE HEAVENLIES 12:7-12

AND THERE WAS WAR IN HEAVEN: MICHAEL AND HIS ANGELS, FOUGHT AGAINST THE DRAGON; AND THE DRAGON FOUGHT AND HIS ANGELS, AND PREVAILED NOT; NEITHER WAS THEIR PLACE FOUND ANY MORE IN HEAVEN. AND THE GREAT DRAGON WAS CAST OUT, THAT OLD SERPENT, CALLED THE DEVIL, AND SATAN, WHICH DECEIVETH THE WHOLE WORLD:

12:13-17 (cf MATT. 24:15-21)

GOD PROVIDES A PLACE OF SAFETY FOR ISRAEL THWARTING SATAN'S INTENT OF DESTRUCTION

AND WHEN THE DRAGON SAW THAT HE WAS CAST UNTO THE EARTH HE PERSECUTED THE WOMAN WHICH BROUGHT FORTH THE MAN CHILD...AND THE WOMAN FLED INTO THE WILDERNESS, WHERE SHE HATH A PLACE PREPARED OF GOD...AND THE EARTH OPENED HER MOUTH, AND SWALLOWED UP THE FLOOD WHICH THE DRAGON (SATAN) CAST OUT OF HIS MOUTH.

RISE OF THE ANTICHRIST 13:1-10

THE SYMBOL

SAYING... "WHO IS LIKE UNTO THE BEAST?" 13:4

...I SAW A BEAST RISE UP OUT OF THE SEA, HAVING SEVEN HEADS AND TEN HORNS AND UPON THE HORNS TEN CROWNS...AND THE DRAGON (SATAN) GAVE HIM HIS POWER, AND HIS THRONE, AND GREAT AUTHORITY... AND THEY WORSHIPPED THE DRAGON...AND THE BEAST...AND ALL THAT DWELL UPON THE EARTH SHALL WORSHIP HIM WHOSE NAMES ARE NOT WRITTEN IN THE BOOK OF LIFE...

CHAPTER 14 CONTAINS A SERIES OF ANTICIPATIVE VISIONS — NOT IN CHRONOLOGICAL ORDER — THE FULFILLMENT IS DESCRIBED IN LATER CHAPTERS

(STUDY 3 - CONTINUED)

RISE OF THE FALSE PROPHET 13:11-18

THE SYMBOL

666

HE CAUSETH ALL TO WORSHIP THE IMAGE OF THE BEAST - 13:15

AND I BEHELD ANOTHER BEAST COMING UP OUT OF THE EARTH; AND HE HAD TWO HORNS LIKE A LAMB, AND HE SPAKE LIKE A DRAGON...AND CAUSE THAT AS MANY AS WOULD NOT WORSHIP THE IMAGE OF THE BEAST SHOULD BE KILLED. AND HE CAUSETH ALL... TO RECEIVE A MARK IN THEIR RIGHT HAND, OR FOREHEAD. THE NUMBER OF THE BEAST IS THE NUMBER OF A MAN. .666.

THE LAMB AND THE 144,000. (14:1-5) ON MOUNT SION (cf. Ps. 2:6)

"AND THEY SUNG, AS IT WERE A NEW SONG"

AND I LOOKED, AND LO, A LAMB STOOD ON THE MOUNT SION, AND WITH HIM AN HUNDRED AND FORTY AND FOUR THOUSAND HAVING HIS FATHER'S NAME WRITTEN IN THEIR FOREHEADS...AND THEY SUNG AS IT WERE A NEW SONG... THAT NO MAN COULD LEARN BUT THE HUNDRED AND FORTY AND FOUR THOUSAND, WHICH WERE REDEEMED FROM THE EARTH...BEING THE FIRSTFRUITS UNTO GOD AND TO THE LAMB

"BABYLON IS FALLEN" (CHAPS. 17-18)

PROCLAMATION OF THE AGELESS GOSPEL 14:6-7

"FEAR GOD AND GIVE HIM GLORY FOR THE HOUR OF JUDGMENT IS COME"

AND I SAW ANOTHER ANGEL FLYING IN THE MIDST OF HEAVEN, HAVING THE EVER-LASTING GOSPEL TO PREACH UNTO THEM THAT DWELL ON THE EARTH...SAYING WITH A LOUD VOICE, FEAR GOD AND GIVE GLORY TO HIM; FOR THE HOUR OF HIS JUDGMENT IS COME: AND THERE FOLLOWED ANOTHER ANGEL, SAYING, BABYLON IS FALLEN! (THE ANTICIPATIVE ANNOUNCE-MENT OF THE FALL OF THAT GREAT CITY)

DOOM OF THE BEAST WORSHIPPERS - 14:9-11

666

THE SAME SHALL DRINK OF THE WINE OF THE WRATH OF GOD" 14:10

AND THE THIRD ANGEL FOLLOWED THEM, SAYING, IF ANY MAN WORSHIP THE BEAST AND HIS IMAGE, AND RECEIVE HIS MARK, THE SAME SHALL DRINK OF THE WRATH OF GOD...AND HE SHALL BE TORMENTED WITH FIRE AND BRIMSTONE IN THE PRESENCE OF THE HOLY ANGELS, AND OF THE LAMB: AND THE SMOKE OF THEIR TORMENT ASCENDETH UP FOR EVER AND EVER...

Cf. MATT. 13:38-43 THE HARVEST AND THE VINTAGE JUDGMENT

THE VISION - 14:14-20 cf: JOEL 3:13 - REV. 19:15.

AND I LOOKED, AND BEHOLD A WHITE CLOUD, AND ON THE CLOUD ONE SAT LIKE UNTO THE SON OF MAN, HAVING ON HIS HEAD A GOLDEN CROWN, AND IN HIS HAND A SHARP SICKLE. AND ANOTHER ANGEL CAME OUT OF THE TEMPLE CRYING, THRUST IN THY SICKLE.. AND REAP... ANOTHER ANGEL CAME, HE ALSO HAVING A SHARP SICKLE...AND GATHERED THE VINE OF THE EARTH AND CAST IT INTO THE WINEPRESS OF THE WRATH OF GOD...

PRELUDE (15:1-4) AND PREPARATION FOR THE VIAL JUDGMENTS 15:5-8

15:2

SEVEN ANGELS HAVING THE SEVEN VIALS OF THE WRATH OF GOD.

AND I SAW AS IT WERE A SEA OF GLASS MINGLED WITH FIRE: AND THEM THAT HAD GOTTEN THE VICTORY OVER THE BEAST... AND THEY SING THE SONG OF MOSES AND OF THE LAMB...AND SEVEN ANGELS CAME OUT OF THE TEMPLE, HAVING THE SEVEN PLAGUES...AND THE TEMPLE WAS FILLED WITH SMOKE...AND NO MAN WAS ABLE TO ENTER TILL THE SEVEN PLAGUES WERE FULFILLED...

STUDY 3 (CONTINUED) "THE THINGS WHICH SHALL BE HEREAFTER"
THE VIAL JUDGMENTS – THE SEVEN LAST PLAGUES

THE FIRST VIAL

16:2
A PLAGUE OF GRIEVOUS SORES

I HEARD A GREAT VOICE OUT OF THE TEMPLE SAYING TO THE SEVEN ANGELS, GO YOUR WAYS AND POUR OUT THE VIALS OF THE WRATH OF GOD UPON THE EARTH. AND THE FIRST WENT, AND POURED OUT HIS VIAL...AND THERE FELL A NOISOME AND GRIEVOUS SORE UPON THE MEN WHICH HAD THE MARK OF THE BEAST, AND UPON THEM WHICH WORSHIPPED HIS IMAGE...

THE SECOND VIAL

16:3
THE SEA TURNED INTO BLOOD

AND THE SECOND ANGEL POURED OUT HIS VIAL UPON THE SEA; AND IT BECAME AS THE BLOOD OF A DEAD MAN AND EVERY LIVING SOUL DIED IN THE SEA.
(GREEK TEXT RENDERING – "IT BECAME BLOOD AS OF [ONE] DEAD"

THE THIRD VIAL

16:4-7
THE FRESH-WATER SYSTEM OF THE EARTH TURNED INTO BLOOD

AND THE THIRD ANGEL POURED OUT HIS VIAL UPON THE RIVERS AND FOUNTAINS OF WATERS; AND THEY BECAME BLOOD...THOU ART RIGHTEOUS O LORD...BECAUSE THOU HAST JUDGED THUS...FOR THEY HAVE SHED THE BLOOD OF SAINTS AND PROPHETS, AND THOU HAST GIVEN THEM BLOOD TO DRINK...

THE FOURTH VIAL

16:8-9
THE SUN TO "SCORCH MEN WITH FIRE"

AND THE FOURTH ANGEL POURED OUT HIS VIAL UPON THE SUN; AND POWER WAS GIVEN HIM TO SCORCH MEN WITH FIRE. AND MEN WERE SCORCHED WITH GREAT HEAT, AND BLASPHEMED THE NAME OF GOD, WHICH HATH POWER OVER THESE PLAGUES: AND THEY REPENTED NOT TO GIVE HIM GLORY...

THE FIFTH VIAL

16:10-11
THE KINGDOM OF THE ANTICHRIST SMITTEN WITH DARKNESS

AND THE FIFTH ANGEL POURED OUT HIS VIAL UPON THE KINGDOM OF THE BEAST: AND HIS KINGDOM WAS FULL OF DARKNESS: AND THEY GNAWED THEIR TONGUES FOR PAIN, AND BLASPHEMED THE GOD OF HEAVEN BECAUSE OF THEIR PAINS AND THEIR SORES, AND REPENTED NOT OF THEIR DEEDS...

THE SIXTH VIAL

16:12-16
DRYING UP OF THE RIVER EUPHRATES

AND THE SIXTH ANGEL POURED OUT HIS VIAL UPON THE GREAT RIVER EUPHRATES AND THE WATER THEREOF WAS DRIED UP, THAT THE WAY OF THE KINGS OF THE EAST MIGHT BE PREPARED...AND HE GATHERED THEM TOGETHER INTO A PLACE CALLED IN THE HEBREW TONGUE ARMAGEDDON...

STUDY 3 (CONTINUED) "THE THINGS WHICH SHALL BE HEREAFTER"

THE SYMBOL

ARMAGEDDON

THE SEVENTH VIAL

"IT IS DONE"

THE SYMBOL

BABYLON IS FALLEN

"COME OUT OF HER MY PEOPLE"

16:13-16

THE EVIL TRINITY SEDUCES KINGS OF THE WORLD TO THE BATTLE OF ARMAGEDDON

AND I SAW THREE UNCLEAN SPIRITS LIKE FROGS COME OUT OF THE MOUTH OF THE DRAGON, THE BEAST, AND THE FALSE PROPHET... FOR THEY ARE THE SPIRITS OF DEVILS, WHICH GO FORTH UNTO THE KINGS OF THE EARTH...TO GATHER THEM TO THE BATTLE OF THAT DAY OF GOD ALMIGHTY... AND HE GATHERED THEM TOGETHER INTO A PLACE CALLED IN THE HEBREW TONGUE ARMAGEDDON.

16:17-21

CONSUMMATION OF THE VIAL JUDGMENTS - WHILE MEN STILL BLASPHEME GOD.

AND THE SEVENTH ANGEL POURED OUT HIS VIAL INTO THE AIR; AND THERE CAME A GREAT VOICE...FROM THE THRONE, SAYING, IT IS DONE. AND THERE WAS A GREAT EARTH-QUAKE...AND THERE FELL FROM HEAVEN UPON MEN A GREAT HAIL, EVERY STONE ABOUT THE WEIGHT OF A TALENT: AND MEN BLASPHEMED GOD BECAUSE OF THE PLAGUE OF THE HAIL; FOR THE PLAGUE WAS EXCEEDING GREAT.

17:1-15

THE GREAT HARLOT. THE APOSTATE RELIGIOUS SYSTEM SUPPORTED BY THE WORLD'S POLITICAL LEADERS

AND THERE CAME ONE OF THE SEVEN ANGELS SAYING UNTO ME, COME HITHER, I WILL SHEW THEE THE JUDGMENT OF THE GREAT WHORE THAT SITTETH UPON MANY WATERS WITH WHOM THE KINGS OF THE EARTH HATH COMMITTED FORNICATION...AND I SAW THE WOMAN DRUNKEN WITH THE BLOOD OF SAINTS AND MARTYRS...AND THE ANGEL SAID...I WILL TELL THEE OF THE MYSTERY OF THE WOMAN, AND THE BEAST THAT CARRIED HER...

18:1-19

THE TEN HORNS (WORLD POWERS) TURN AGAINST ECCLESIASTICAL BABYLON, TO HER DESTRUCTION.

AFTER THESE THINGS I SAW ANOTHER ANGEL COME DOWN FROM HEAVEN...AND THE EARTH WAS LIGHTENED WITH HIS GLORY. AND HE CRIED BABYLON THE GREAT IS FALLEN... (18:1-8). AND THE TEN HORNS SHALL HATE THE WHORE...AND BURN HER WITH FIRE. AND THE WOMAN IS THAT GREAT CITY, WHICH REIGNETH OVER THE KINGS OF THE EARTH (17:16-18) AND THE KINGS AND MERCHANTS SHALL WEEP AND MOURN OVER HER (18:9-19)

18:20-24

AS THE ANGEL CASTS A GREAT MILLSTONE INTO THE SEA; THUS SHALL BE BABYLON'S DOOM.

REJOICE OVER HER, THOU HEAVEN, AND YE HOLY APOSTLES AND PROPHETS; FOR GOD HATH AVENGED YOU ON HER. AND A MIGHTY ANGEL TOOK UP A STONE LIKE A GREAT MILLSTONE; AND CAST IT INTO THE SEA, SAYING, THUS WITH VIOLENCE SHALL THAT GREAT CITY BABYLON BE THROWN DOWN, AND SHALL BE FOUND NO MORE AT ALL.

STUDY 3 (CONTINUED) "THE THINGS WHICH SHALL BE HEREAFTER"

19:1-10
THE MARRIAGE OF THE LAMB

AND THE FOUR AND TWENTY ELDERS AND THE FOUR LIVING CREATURES FELL DOWN AND WORSHIPPED GOD THAT SAT ON THE THRONE. AND I HEARD A GREAT MULTITUDE SAYING,...ALLELUIA, THE LORD GOD OMNIPOTENT REIGNETH. LET US REJOICE, AND GIVE HONOR TO HIM: FOR THE MARRIAGE OF THE LAMB IS COME, AND HIS WIFE HATH MADE HERSELF READY, AND TO HER WAS GRANTED THAT SHE SHOULD BE ARRAYED IN FINE LINEN...THE RIGHTEOUSNESS OF THE SAINTS. BLESSED ARE THEY WHICH ARE CALLED UNTO THE MARRIAGE SUPPER OF THE LAMB...

19:11-21. 20:1-3
THE BATTLE OF ARMAGEDDON and THE SECOND COMING OF CHRIST IN GLORY. cf. MATT. 24:27-31, DAN. 2:35

19:17-18

THE LAKE OF FIRE   THE PIT

AND I SAW HEAVEN OPEN AND BEHOLD A WHITE HORSE AND HE THAT SAT UPON HIM WAS CALLED FAITHFUL AND TRUE, AND IN RIGHTEOUSNESS DOTH HE JUDGE AND MAKE WAR...AND THE ARMIES WHICH FOLLOWED HIM UPON WHITE HORSES WERE CLOTHED IN FINE LINEN; AND OUT OF HIS MOUTH WENT A SHARP SWORD, THAT WITH IT HE SHOULD SMITE THE NATIONS...AND HE HATH UPON HIS VESTURE A NAME WRITTEN, KING OF KINGS AND LORD OF LORDS. I SAW AN ANGEL STANDING IN THE SUN, AND HE CRIED, SAYING TO ALL THE FOWLS THAT FLY, COME, GATHER TOGETHER UNTO THE SUPPER OF THE GREAT GOD. THE BEAST WAS TAKEN AND THE FALSE PROPHET...THESE WERE CAST ALIVE INTO A LAKE OF FIRE...AND AN ANGEL LAID HOLD OF THE DEVIL AND CAST HIM INTO THE BOTTOMLESS PIT FOR A THOUSAND YEARS...

20:5
"BUT THE REST OF THE DEAD LIVED NOT AGAIN UNTIL THE THOUSAND YEARS WERE FINISHED. THIS IS THE FIRST RESURRECTION."

AND I SAW THRONES, AND THEY SAT UPON THEM, AND JUDGMENT WAS GIVEN THEM: AND I SAW THE SOULS OF THEM THAT WERE BEHEADED FOR THE WITNESS OF JESUS...BLESSED AND HOLY IS HE THAT HATH PART IN THE FIRST RESURRECTION: ON SUCH THE SECOND DEATH HATH NO POWER, BUT THEY SHALL BE PRIESTS OF GOD AND OF CHRIST AND SHALL REIGN WITH HIM A THOUSAND YEARS...

KING OF KINGS AND LORD OF LORDS

HOLINESS UNTO THE LORD
ZECH. 14:20

EZK. 47:12
ZECH. 14:8

MICAH 4:4   ISA. 65:21

REV. 20:6
CHRIST'S REIGN OF A THOUSAND YEARS - WITH HIS SAINTS.

HE SHALL HAVE DOMINION UNTO THE ENDS OF THE EARTH, ALL KINGS SHALL FALL BEFORE HIM; ALL NATIONS SHALL SERVE HIM.
BLESSED AND HOLY IS HE THAT HATH PART IN THE FIRST RESURRECTION...THEY SHALL BE PRIESTS OF GOD AND OF CHRIST, AND SHALL REIGN WITH HIM A THOUSAND YEARS.
IF WE SUFFER WE SHALL ALSO REIGN WITH HIM.
FOR THOU WAST SLAIN, AND HAST REDEEMED US BY THY BLOOD...AND HAST MADE US KINGS AND PRIESTS AND WE SHALL REIGN ON THE EARTH.

STUDY 3 (CONTINUED) "THE THINGS WHICH SHALL BE HEREAFTER"

AND WHOSOEVER WAS NOT FOUND WRITTEN IN THE BOOK OF LIFE WAS CAST INTO THE LAKE OF FIRE.

REV. 20:15

SATAN LOOSED FROM THE PIT. 20:7-9

AND WHEN THE THOUSAND YEARS ARE FINISHED, SATAN SHALL BE LOOSED OUT OF HIS PRISON AND SHALL GO OUT TO DECEIVE THE NATIONS...AND SHALL GATHER THEM TO BATTLE...AND THEY COMPASSED THE BELOVED CITY, AND FIRE CAME DOWN FROM GOD OUT OF HEAVEN, AND DEVOURED THEM. AND THE DEVIL WAS CAST INTO THE LAKE OF FIRE, WHERE THE BEAST AND THE FALSE PROPHET ARE, AND SHALL BE TORMENTED DAY AND NIGHT FOR EVER AND EVER.

THE REST OF THE DEAD 20:11-15   **THE 20:10 LAKE OF FIRE**

AND I SAW A GREAT WHITE THRONE, AND HIM THAT SAT ON IT...AND I SAW THE DEAD, SMALL AND GREAT, STAND BEFORE GOD; AND THE BOOKS WERE OPENED: AND ANOTHER BOOK WAS OPENED WHICH IS THE BOOK OF LIFE: AND THE DEAD WERE JUDGED OUT OF THOSE THINGS WHICH WERE WRITTEN IN THE BOOKS, ACCORDING TO THEIR WORKS. AND WHOSO-EVER WAS NOT FOUND WRITTEN IN THE BOOK OF LIFE WAS CAST INTO THE LAKE OF FIRE.

21:1-8 A NEW HEAVEN – A NEW EARTH AND THE NEW JERUSALEM.

AND I SAW A NEW HEAVEN AND A NEW EARTH: FOR THE FIRST HEAVEN AND THE FIRST EARTH WERE PASSED AWAY AND THERE WAS NO MORE SEA; AND I JOHN SAW THE HOLY CITY, NEW JERUSALEM, COMING DOWN FROM GOD OUT OF HEAVEN, PREPARED AS A BRIDE ADORNED FOR HER HUSBAND. AND I HEARD A GREAT VOICE OUT OF HEAVEN SAYING, BEHOLD, THE TABERNACLE OF GOD IS WITH MEN... BEHOLD, I MAKE ALL THINGS NEW...IT IS DONE. HE THAT OVERCOMETH SHALL INHERIT ALL THINGS: I WILL BE HIS GOD, AND HE SHALL BE MY SON.

MATTHEW MARK LUKE   JOHN PETER PAUL

21:9-27, 22:1-7 "I WILL SHEW THEE THE BRIDE -THE LAMB'S WIFE" Vss. 9-10

THERE CAME UNTO ME ONE OF THE SEVEN ANGELS SAYING, COME, HITHER, I WILL SHEW THEE THE BRIDE, THE LAMB'S WIFE. AND HE CARRIED ME IN THE SPIRIT TO A HIGH MOUNTAIN, AND SHEWED ME THAT GREAT CITY, THE HOLY JERUSALEM, DESCEND-ING OUT OF HEAVEN FROM GOD, HAVING THE GLORY OF GOD...AND I SAW NO TEMPLE THEREIN FOR THE LORD GOD ALMIGHTY AND THE LAMB ARE THE TEMPLE OF IT. AND THE CITY HAD NO NEED OF SUN NOR MOON TO SHINE IN IT. FOR THE GLORY OF GOD DID LIGHTEN IT, AND THE LAMB IS THE LIGHT THEREOF.

I AM ALPHA AND OMEGA THE BEGINNING AND THE END, THE FIRST AND THE LAST...

I AM THE ROOT AND THE OFFSPRING OF DAVID AND THE BRIGHT AND MORNING STAR...

THE SPIRIT AND THE BRIDE SAY, COME...LET HIM THAT IS ATHIRST COME ···AND WHOSOEVER WILL LET HIM TAKE OF THE WATER OF LIFE FREELY...

SURELY I COME QUICKLY. AMEN EVEN SO, COME LORD JESUS

THE LAST MESSAGE OF GOD'S HOLY WORD 22:8-21

her desolate and naked, and shall eat her flesh, and burn her with fire" (17:16). The Beast (the Antichrist) and the confederate kings join in their hatred of the great ecclesiastical harlot. Realizing that the ecumenical superchurch has used her political power and influence to seduce and intoxicate the world and entrench herself as the governing and controlling power.

The time is come in God's long suffering patience for her destruction. Thus, He put it in the hearts of the political leaders to turn upon her in their hate and to destroy her. The enemies of the true church become God's instruments in executing judgment upon the false apostate system of religious Babylon. The fate of the instruments themselves and of the great political world power personified by the Antichrist (the last blasphemous world ruler and dictator), is reserved for total destruction at the coming of the Lord who "shall smite the earth with the rod of his mouth, and with the breath of his lips shall he slay the wicked" (Isaiah 11:4; Revelation 19:15).

THE FALL OF BABYLON

The title "MYSTERY, BABYLON THE GREAT," which has been our brief subject of study, is one of the most difficult portions of the Apocalypse for the student to follow with absolute clarity. Even the most learned expositors differ in their analysis of its complexities. Keep in mind the two different aspects of Babylon: **First**, as the original fountainhead of Babylonian religion of mystic and idolatrous rites, and its influence on the religious and political world systems throughout church history—culminating in the apostate ecumenical monstrosity symbolized as the Mother of Harlots; and, **second**, as a literal city viewed in its political, economic and commercial aspects, for kings and merchants of the earth mourn its destruction, as they wax rich through the abundance of her merchandise.

The great difficulty is to try to condense such a far reaching subject, and it is even more difficult to pin-point the meaningful events by the visual approach of illustration such as the author-artist attempts in this Panorama. Therefore, it is presented not dogmatically but with a hope and a prayer that it may be an aid to stimulate the imagination with a clearer concept of this timely subject.

In chapter 17:1-18 we viewed the collapse and destruction of the ecclesiastical power symbolized as the Great Harlot, arrayed in purple and scarlet and bedecked with ornamental trappings of great wealth. This could well be, primarily, a picture of the Roman Church, but in the end picture it is the culmination of apostate Romanism, Protestantism and all the apostate isms with the accumulated wealth of *organized religion,*—synonymous with power.

Chapter 18 begins with the words "After these things" denoting a new aspect in Babylon's judgment. J. A. Seis, in his *Apocalypse,* notes "two separate stages of the fall answering to the two aspects in which Babylon is contemplated, referring first to Babylon in mystery, as a system of false worship, and second to Babylon as a city, in which this system is finally embodied."

The announcement of Babylon's downfall is made by another angel whose brightness enlightened the satanic scene of Babylon's corruption. The angel cried mightily, "Babylon the great is fallen, is fallen, and is become the habitation of devils . . . and every foul spirit" (18:1-2). Her corrupt influence is again stated in 18:3. In verses 4 to 8 a voice from heaven is heard appealing to God's people—in this instance the tribulation saints and those turning to God in the midst of the woes. This appeal is also applicable to believers even today to come out from among them for the Christian is in this world but not of the world.

Chapter 18:9-19 describes the weeping of those trafficking in the abundant merchandise of the mighty city while all heaven rejoices, marvelling, no doubt, at God's long-suffering and the righteousness of His vengeance (18:20).

"And a mighty angel took up a stone like a great millstone, and cast it into the sea, saying, Thus with violence shall that great city Babylon be thrown down, and shall be found no more at all" (verse 21). The remaining verses of the chapter, with dramatic emphasis, describe the ominous picture of desolation. No more music, no workers, no grinding of the millstone, no lights, no happiness, and the chapter closes with a grim reminder of the bloody character of her infamous system (18:1-24).

CHART NO. 12

THE MARRIAGE OF THE LAMB AND THE SECOND COMING OF CHRIST (chapter 19).

Again chapter 19 begins with "After these things" denoting another event in the unfolding panorama—a glorious, long awaited, heavenly event preceded by the Alleluias of the glorified saints praising God for His righteous judgments. Now that the great Harlot is judged and destroyed, the true Bride, awaiting in heaven, can now be brought forth in all of her beauty. She is arrayed not in purple and scarlet bedecked with earth's ornaments but "in fine linen, clean and white: for the fine linen is the righteousness of the saints" (19:8).

John, no doubt overcome with spiritual ecstasy, writes, "And I heard as it were the voice of a great multitude . . . saying, Alleluia: for the Lord God omnipotent reigneth. Let us be glad and rejoice, and give honour to him: for the marriage of the Lamb is come, and his wife hath made herself ready" (19:7). *The Lamb's wife* is *the Bride* (21:9), the true church—all born-again, glorified saints embraced from Pentecost to the Rapture.

The Marriage, of which no details are given, is a heavenly event taking place on the eve of Christ's returning to the earth to rule and to reign in righteousness. The Bridegroom is the Lamb, the Redeemer who ". . . loved the church, and gave himself for it" (Ephesians 5:25).

In the New Testament, the church is the Bride of Christ—the marriage of the Lamb, the blessed consummation of God's purpose "in the beloved." Christ, in the character of the Lamb, acknowledges and takes unto Himself, as co-heirs of His Throne, all those chosen ones who have been faithful in their betrothal, who now, as the Lamb's Bride, reign with Him and share His blessed inheritance forever.

This glorious event is the consummation of the Divine purpose in this present age. With the outpouring of the Holy Spirit at Pentecost it was announced that "God at the first [literally, for the first time] did visit the Gentiles, to take out of them a people for his name" (Acts 15:14). The taking out of a people is distinctly the work and purpose of God in this present dispensation of Grace. The outcalling of the church (Greek *ekklesia*), an assembly of hell-deserving sinners redeemed by the blood of the Lamb, is the eternal manifestation of the infinite grace of God, "That in the ages to come he might shew the exceeding riches of his grace in his kindness toward us through Christ Jesus" (Ephesians 2:7).

THE MARRIAGE SUPPER (19:9).

The marriage supper, according to traditional arrangement, follows the marriage, so it is that "they which are called unto the marriage supper of the Lamb" are the invited guests. The guests are naturally distinguished from the Bride. The question, Who are the invited guests who attend the marriage supper with the special blessing of God?, is still debated even among theologians. One seemingly logical answer is that the guests are the Old Testament Saints (for no one was baptized into the *one body* (1 Corinthians 12:12-13; Galatians 3:27-28) before Pentecost.

It is suggested that John the Baptist, who died before the crucifixion of Christ, will be a guest at the supper as the friend of the bridegroom. For regarding his own relationship John says, "He that hath the bride is the bridegroom: but the friend of the bridegroom, that standeth and heareth him, rejoiceth greatly because of the bridegroom's voice: this my joy therefore is fulfilled" (John 3:29). This should give light to part of the question.

Jesus (the Bridegroom) testified: "Among them that are born of woman there hath not risen a greater than John the Baptist." He is not, however, by his own testimony, of the Bride but the friend of the bridegroom. Of this we are assured, they all are redeemed by the blood of the Lamb, whether looking forward to the altar of the slain Lamb of God in anticipation or looking back to the eternal sacrifice on Calvary's cross, and all are called *Blessed,* for the angel said, "These are the true sayings of God" (19:9).

THE SECOND COMING OF CHRIST IN GLORY (19:11-16).

"And I saw heaven opened, and behold a white horse; and he that sat upon him was called Faithful and True, and in righteousness he doth judge and make war. His eyes were as a flame of fire, and on His head were many crowns; and he had a name written, that no one knew, but he himself. And he was clothed with a vesture dipped in blood: and his name is called the Word of God."

Here we realize clearly the full import of the title of our study—The Revelation, or Apocalypse—the actual personal appearance, a literal manifestation, the unveiling of our Lord Jesus Christ. Christ is revealed to mortal view when "every eye shall see him." In 2 Thessalonians 2:8 Paul speaks of that wicked [one] "whom the Lord shall consume with the spirit (Greek *pneuma*, breath) of his mouth and destroy with the brightness of his coming." The Greek word *parousia*, translated *coming* denotes personal presence—the literal, bodily appearing of Christ. The word *epiphaneia* translated *brightness*, is literally *appearing*—emphasizing the truth that Christ will actually appear and be seen, and His Glory manifested.

John beholds heaven opened for our Lord's glorious descent with power and great glory (Matthew 24:27-31). As the heavenly attendants assured the watching disciples at Christ's ascension, " . . . this same Jesus, which is taken up from you into heaven, shall so come in like manner as ye have seen him go into heaven," literally, bodily and visibly, so shall he descend from heaven in like manner

The manner of Christ's coming is revealed as twofold in character. He is coming **for** His church and **with** His church—and between the twofold purpose of the glorious event, there will be a relatively short interval during which momentous and climactic events will take place both in heaven and on the earth. The unfolding panorama of these events has been the theme of our study of the Book of Revelation. The pivotal points of our study, around which all revolves, are: (1) John beholds "A door opened in heaven," and a voice inviting him to "Come up hither"; (2) "I saw heaven opened, and behold a white horse; and he that sat upon him was called Faithful and True . . . "; (3) **Chapter 4 begins the third division of the book.** The first division was "The things which thou has seen" (chapter 1). The second division was "The things which are" (chapters 2 and 3). The third and prophetic division was "The things which shall be hereafter." Everything from chapter 4 to chapter 22 is divinely predicted to be fulfilled after the church is taken from the earthly scene.

Thus, the opening of the door in heaven has close association with the Rapture. Then followed the momentous events and the outpouring of God's wrath upon the rebellious earth-dwellers, until in chapter 19:11 again John sees "heaven opened"—this time to publicly make manifest the King of kings and Lord of lords descending from heaven with power and great glory, accompanied by His glorified saints and the holy angels. Thus, the first open door in heaven is suggestive of Christ coming for His people, and the second time heaven is opened Christ is coming with His people, and in between momentous events occur that have to do with the Apocalyptic judgments. Up to chapter 19 the judgments have been directed from heaven with the angels carrying out their execution. Now, Christ descends to earth in person for the final execution of judgment upon the Satan-inspired conspirators and the leaders of the darkness of this world.

"And the armies which were in heaven followed him upon white horses, clothed in fine linen, white and clean." This, we are told, is "the righteousness of the saints." Then, this question may arise: how did they get to heaven to return with the Lord? The answer is, like any other army, they were mobilized —"For the Lord himself shall descend from heaven with a shout, with the voice of the archangel, and with the trump of God [the bugle call]: and the dead in Christ shall rise first: Then we which are alive and remain shall be caught up together with them in the clouds, to meet the Lord in the air: and so shall we ever be with the Lord" (1 Thessalonians 4:16-17). Thus, there is no mistaking their identity; they are the ransomed, raptured church of the Firstborn, The Bride of the Lamb, now returning to the earthly scene with her Lord as warrior, Judge, and King. They need no bucklers, shields or armor for, with glorified bodies like unto her Lord (Philippians 3:21; Romans 8:17), earth's carnal weapons can harm them no more (1 John 3:2).

The coming King rides with regal majesty upon a white horse (verse 11). He came the first time meek and lowly riding upon "a colt the foal of an ass," but in His glorious epiphany His martial charger is symbolical of majesty, righteousness and justice. He, whose vesture is dipped in blood, bears the only weapon against the accumulated weaponry of the armies of the earth—a sharp sword (verse 15). By the sword which "proceedeth out of his mouth" they perish (verse 21).

THE BATTLE OF ARMAGEDDON (19:17-21).

"And I saw an angel standing in the sun; and he cried with a loud voice, saying to all the fowls that fly in the midst of heaven, Come and gather yourselves together unto the supper of the great God" (19:17). Standing in the sun, where he could be seen by all, the angel invites the ravenous birds in the heavens, in anticipation of certain victory by the King of kings, to come and eat the flesh of kings, horses and all men great and small until they are filled with their flesh.

"And I [John] saw the beast, and the kings of the earth, and their armies, gathered together to make war . . . against his army" (verse 19). The greatest combination of powers of earth and Hell ever witnessed is gathered "to the battle of that great day of God Almighty" (16:14)—war against God and His Christ. Take note again who is engaged in the conflict: the Beast (the Antichrist) acclaimed by the world its invincible leader with the combined armies of the kings of the earth, and their opponent, He that sitteth upon the white horse and His armies which were with Him in heaven. This war, unlike all other wars, is not an array of nation against nation, race against race, but the gathering climax of God's declared *enmity* of Genesis 3:15—the seed of the serpent, Antichrist and his followers, and the seed of the woman, Christ and those that are His. No details of the battle are given, for actually there is no battle. We are simply assured that "The Lamb shall overcome them," and " . . . he shall smite the earth with the rod of his mouth, and with the breath of his lips he shall slay the wicked" (Isaiah 11:4; Revelation 19:15).

The sovereignty of the earth, already decreed in the mind and purpose of God (Psalm 2), is settled forever before three worlds: Heaven, Earth and Hell.

The bloody holocast of World War 1 was designated by deluded optimists as the war to end war. But soon the earth staggered under the throes of another bloodbath unequaled in barbarism and lust for power. There will not be peace until the Prince of Peace shall come in righteousness to make war. This sounds paradoxical, but when Christ comes to meet the satanic trio's armies in open and conclusive conflict, **this will be the only war in the blood-soaked history of the world in which the outcome will abolish war forever in the earth by God's sacred promise** (Isaiah 2:4).

THE FATE OF THE SATANIC TRINITY (19:20-21).

"And the beast (the Antichrist) was taken, and with him the false prophet. . . . These both were cast alive into a lake of fire burning with brimstone [which was] . . . prepared for the devil and his angels" (Matthew 25:41). The self-acclaimed god, whose worshipers held to be invincible,—the leader of the God-defiant world order and commander-in-chief of earth's amassed military might energized by Satan—is now taken and none can help him. He is cast down never to arise again and with him the false prophet who worked satanic miracles and was the personification of all ecclesiastical evil and heresy. They were cast into the final *gehenna*, Hell, the place of the eternally damned, into which none have yet entered, until the final judgment of the wicked dead at the Great White Throne (19:20; 20:11-15).

"The remnant [of earth's armies] were slain with the sword of him that sat upon the horse . . . and all the fowls were filled with their flesh." A banquet supper, indeed, for the hovering vultures.

THE BINDING OF SATAN (20:1-3).

"And I saw an angel come down from heaven, having the key of the bottomless pit and a great chain in his hand. And he laid hold on the dragon, that old serpent, which is the Devil, and Satan, and bound him a thousand years. And cast him into the bottomless pit, and shut him up, and set a seal upon him, that he should deceive the nations no more, till the thousand years should be fulfilled; and after that he must be loosed for a little season." With the two infamous leaders consigned to their doom, and the slain of the remnant of the armies becoming carrion for the fowls of the air, there is yet the other malignant power, he who is the instigator of the mad conspiracy to make war against the King of kings—the age-old deceiver of men and nations, with whom God at last deals in righteous retribution. The principal character is the master-mind behind the world's blasphemous rebellion against the only mediator between a loving God and sinful man (1 Timothy 2:5). Satan, bent on thwarting "the seed of the woman" from becoming "King of all the earth," is seized and bound and cast into the pit, or abyss, laid hold upon (Greek *ekratese*, denoting quick seizure by strength and force). Although Satan is a malignant spirit, he is also a personal devil. The key and the chain by which he is bound, even if symbolical, signify the sovereignty of God over the denizens of the pit and nether regions.

Thus, ends the present Satan-dominated world system. The earth, at last, shall be free from Satan's sinister presence and deceptive influence for a thousand years. It only remains to tell of his final perdition " . . . when the thousand years should be fulfilled."

THE FIRST RESURRECTION (20:4–6).

"And I saw thrones, and they that sat upon them, and judgment was given them: and I saw the souls of them that were beheaded for the witness of Jesus, and for the word of God . . . and they lived and reigned with Christ a thousand years."

When the seventh angel sounded the seventh trumpet he declared, in certain anticipation, "The kingdoms of this world are become the kingdoms of our Lord, and of his Christ; and he shall reign for ever and ever." The *Revised Version* substitutes *The Kingdom* (singular)—thus a better reading would be "The World-Kingdom of our Lord and of his Christ is come." (Revelation 11:15.)

The scene of the angel's announcement was prophetic. But in the vision before us (although still prophetic) it is, as John sees it, actually *come*, and verses 4 to 6 contain a summary of the saints who, it is written, shall share in Christ's reign of righteousness. John first recorded seeing thrones and to those who sat upon them, judgment was given. *They* are most assuredly the glorified saints, made "kings and priests unto God" and the fulfillment of the Holy Spirit's words, "Do ye not know that the Saints shall judge the world?" (1 Corinthians 6:2). Then John saw a particular group of martyrs who were beheaded for the witness of Christ. These are identical with the souls of the martyrs seen previously by John in the opening of the fifth seal.

John also speaks of those who had not worshiped the beast upon penalty of death. "And they lived and reigned with Christ a thousand years. . . . This is the first resurrection." In connection with the first resurrection, and those who shall participate, we are reminded of the words of Paul: "But now is Christ risen from the dead, and become the firstfruits of them that slept . . . but every man in his own order . . . ." All having part in the first resurrection are called "Blessed and Holy," and shall share the reign of Christ in whatever capacity their blessing affords. For it seems that some reign, and others serve while sharing in the reign (Revelation 7:14–17). But to God be the glory, He doeth all things well.

"But the rest of the dead lived not again [were not resurrected] until the thousand years were finished" (20:5).

CHRIST'S MILLENNIAL (1000 YEARS) KINGDOM.

The prophets of God throughout the ages have foretold of a glorious era when the Kingdom of God shall be established on the earth in visible glory and righteousness. A kingdom which shall fill the whole earth and shall never be destroyed (Daniel 2:31–45). It is evident that, if this coming kingdom of heavenly rule is to take the place of all previous dominions in the earth (Daniel 2:44), it must be a real, visible, tangible kingdom with a King, a form of government and subjects over whom the King shall rule. It should be just as real a kingdom as those that preceded it, but with one wonderful difference, it will be righteous in character and in government (Psalm 72; Matthew 6:10). It will be, at last, the only true universal Kingdom in world history—not only universal but eternal. All lines of Scripture lead us to the King and the establishment of His Kingdom.

THE SUBJECTS OF CHRIST'S KINGDOM.

The subjects of Christ's Millennial Kingdom will include the remnant of the tested, tried and converted national Israel who survived the refining fires of the great Tribulation and spoken of in the prophetic Scriptures as "the time of Jacob's trouble" (Jeremiah chapter 30), together with the spared, judged, sifted and saved among the Gentile nations (7:9–10).

The host of the slain at Armageddon are not the nations in their entirety but the confederated kings and their armies. After the destruction of the battlefield, "The rod of iron rule" of the conqueror follows. This doesn't mean tyrannical dictatorship as we think of iron rule, but inflexible justice, moral discipline and direction toward a new world government founded upon righteousness—"Thy Kingdom come." At last the prayers of the saints of all ages is fulfilled. The seed of the woman will have bruised the serpent's head, that is, destroyed his headship. The Usurper having been overthrown "the government shall be upon his [Christ's] shoulder." The swords of the nations shall be beaten into plowshares, and there shall be war no more (Isaiah 2:4). The earth, which now groans under the thralldom of the curse (Genesis 3:14–19), shall be restored to Edenic beauty, and the land shall yield its fulness. The Jewish question has long been the perplexing problem of the centuries. Israel, once a proverb, a byword, a curse among the nations (Zechariah 8:13), now restored and redeemed as a nation at Christ's coming, shall be a channel of blessing and evangelization among the nations, in the Kingdom of their long rejected Messiah (Zechariah 8:23).

Author's note: For a full study, together with a visual, illustrated panorama of the Second Coming of Christ and the glory and greatness of the Kingdom of God traced from Genesis to Revelation, see the author's *Panorama No 3. The Second Coming of Christ.*

CHART NO. 13

AN ETERNAL DOOM OF SATAN (20:7–10).

"And when the thousand years are expired, Satan shall be loosed out of his prison." At the end of the thousand years of peace on earth under the direct and righteous administration of the King of kings, Satan is loosed "for a little season," and immediately his evil influence is manifested once more among the nations. He quickly fans the age-old flame of revolt against God and His Christ. It must be remembered that the subjects of the Millennial kingdom are not *glorified* beings, as the saints of the first resurrection, therefore those born during the Millennium will have the same Adamic nature as their fathers but without the external source of temptation—the evil power of satanic suggestion. While Satan is confined to the pit, man the earth dweller is as a keg of dynamite without the spark to set it off. But with Satan loosened from his prison, the spark of rebellious hate touches off the last desperately mad attempt to dethrone the King of kings and thwart God's purpose of a Kingdom of righteousness on earth. **But persistent rebellion against God is death!** God's answer to the rebel's last defiance is told in one short but terribly conclusive sentence: " . . . fire came down from God out of heaven, and devoured them" (20:9).

"And the devil that deceived them was cast into the lake of fire and brimstone, where the beast and the false prophet are, and shall be tormented day and night forever and ever" (20:10). With the last rebellion put down, and the earth, for the first time in human history populated with the righteous only, the great archenemy is utterly foiled and defeated in his blasphemous ambition "to be like God" (Isaiah 14:14) and now meets his final and everlasting perdition. The long awaited sentence is swiftly executed. He is cast into the lake of fire already prepared for him and his blinded and deluded followers. **Thus, ends the last rebellion of a creature against his creator.**

THE JUDGMENT OF THE WICKED DEAD (20:11–15).

"And I saw a great white throne . . . and I saw the dead . . . stand before God; and the books were opened: and another book . . . which is the book of life: and the dead were judged out of those things which were written in the books, according to their works. And whosoever was not found written in the book of life was cast into the lake of fire." Both the Old Testament and the New declare a day of judgment for every individual human being that ever lived and died, from the beginning of the world (*cosmos*) until the end—" . . . it is appointed unto men once to die, but after this the judgment" (Hebrews 9:27). This divine decree is irrevocable in its nature and will determine the eternal destiny of every mortal soul either to everlasting blessedness or everlasting punishment.

The teaching and expression "General Judgment" is nowhere found in the Bible. There is a resurrection of life and a resurrection of damnation, that is, condemnation (John 5:29). These two resurrections could not possibly be one and the same for we are assured that "There is therefore now no condemnation to them that which are in Christ Jesus . . . " (Romans 8:1). The first resurrection is "out from among the dead," and it is necessarily eclectic (selective). Some are resurrected while others are not (1 Thessalonians 4:16; Revelation 20:5–6). "The dead in Christ shall rise first," clearly denotes a rising *out of* or *from among* the unredeemed multitudes not *in Christ*.

In Revelation 20:5 they are referred to as "the rest of the dead." They "lived not again [were not resurrected] until the thousand years were finished." While those of the first resurrection "lived and reigned with Christ" during the thousand years (Christ's

Millennial Reign) "the rest of the dead" remained in their graves. These are associated facts.

THE JUDGMENT AT THE GREAT WHITE THRONE (20:11–15).

The subjects of the Great White Throne Judgment are "the rest of the dead," now resurrected after "the thousand years" (20:5). They stand before the judgment throne; although physically alive they are called "the dead," never having been made alive in Jesus Christ. For " . . . he that hath not the Son of God, hath not life." They are still spiritually dead.

The basis of their judgment is their rejection of the only Saviour and mediator, God's own Son, who loved them and died to save them from sin, spiritual death, and the judgment they now must face.

The books are opened; these are the records of all the deeds of those who have died in their sins. What a blessed assurance to know, that when a sinner turns from his unbelief with a repentant heart and accepts the salvation made possible by the sacrificial death of Jesus Christ, the sinner's record of guilt is blotted out from *the books*, and his name is written in "the book of life." The Book of Life is a record of names not deeds.

In the Apocalyptic vision, as God swung back the curtain (as it were) that veils the future and eternal state and gave John, the Seer, a glimpse of the gathering crescendo of Divine Wrath (the final judgment of the wicked), John recorded the awesome consummation of the scene before him in one terrible sentence of Divine finality: "Whosoever was not found written in the book of life was cast into the lake of fire." Such is the awful and eternal doom and destiny of *the lost*.

The preparation for the Eternal state. The destruction of Satan and the last rebellious earth dwellers; the judgment of the resurrected wicked dead; the purging of every trace of sin and discord in the universe; these are the momentous end-of-time events which mark the preparation for the eternal state. This is the Millennial Kingdom of the Son, with the ransomed saints sharing His reign of righteousness (having fulfilled its divine purpose—the exhibition of the restoration of Divine Sovereignty in the earth being accomplished by the final overthrow of the kingdom of Satan, and the eternal destruction of the usurper). "Then cometh the end, when he [Christ] shall have delivered up the [Millennial] kingdom to God, even the Father . . . that God may be all in all" (1 Corinthians 15:24–28).

THE ETERNAL STATE.

In our study of the Book of Revelation we have followed the course of **the church, Israel and the Gentile nations**. This covers the whole scope of the human race in God's purpose. The church, although now a heavenly people, is made up of both Jew and Gentile; a new creation in Christ Jesus. The Panorama has carried us through our present age into the Millennial Kingdom of a thousand years of righteousness on earth. The age-old enmity between the good and evil forces is past, and now John is given a glimpse into the perfect and eternal state.

After the scene at the Great White Throne (a scene outside of time and beyond human history), we, in vision, are ushered once again into the eternal ages. This is where we began as we opened our Bibles and read the first majestic utterance, "**In the beginning God. . . .**" We were introduced immediately to Elohim, the mighty Author and Cause. And now, in the final chapter we stand spellbound, looking out over the eternal vista of God's glorious tomorrow.

The concluding chapter carries us out beyond finite understanding—we are on the threshold of the infinite. The Great White Throne in the pure blinding whiteness of naked omnipotence—the elements melting with fervent heat—the earth below ablaze with purging, purifying fire (2 Peter 3:10)—above the blue a city coming down from God out of heaven, bringing release from pain and sorrow, death and tears forever (21:1–4)—surely this must be the glorious consummation of all the cherished hopes of the redeemed of the ages. But the seeming end is actually the beginning, for God lets the curtain fall upon time and all things past, declaring: "Former things are passed away." Throwing open wide the portals of the perfect and eternal state, He announces the soul-thrilling declaration that the whole disturbed universe has been hoping, waiting, longing, striving, living and dying to hear, "**BEHOLD I MAKE ALL THINGS NEW.**"

NEW HEAVENS AND A NEW EARTH (21:1–8).

"And I saw a new heaven and a new earth:" (21:1). " . . . Wherein the heavens being on fire shall be dissolved, and the elements shall melt with fervent heat? Nevertheless we, according to his promise, look for new heavens and a new earth, wherein dwelleth righteousness" (2 Peter 3:12–13). The *heavens* and the *earth* designate the respective spheres of the *Saved*—both the heavenly and the earthly peoples of God—wherein righteousness shall *dwell*.

Such passages speak of the earth *passing away* (Greek *parerchomai*), *having fled, perishing*, or *being dissolved*, but never signify annihilation or cessation of being; the idea is transition not extinction. The teaching of Bible revelation assures us that "The earth abideth forever" (Ecclesiastes 1:14; Psalm 119:90; Isaiah 66:22). Put it in the crucible to be purged, changed, cleansed of the old corruption and made anew; that is, the state of things once present is made *to pass away, perish, be dissolved*, to give place to a new, abiding, better and eternal state. Peter writes that the world once before *perished*, but the translated word *world* is cosmos, *order, arrangement, inhabitableness;* as a planet it remained and still exists.

When a man becomes *a new creature*, or *a new creation*, he is not annihilated but changed, "old things pass away, all things become new." The word is *regeneration* (Greek *palingenesis*), *re-creation, making new* (Titus 3:5). "The word signifies a renovation of all visible things when the old is passed away, and heaven and earth are become new" (International Standard Bible Encyclopedia). The *dissolving* spoken of by Peter is the same word used by Jesus regarding Lazarus *(loose him)*, and other instances where the idea of *loosing* is used as *setting free* (Matthew 21:2; Revelation 9:14; 20:7; 1 Corinthians 7:27), the idea being deliverance not destruction (Seiss). A world "wherein dwelleth righteousness" would be a new world, even without any physical change at all (Cambridge Bible).

THE NEW JERUSALEM (21:2, 9–27).

"And I John saw the holy city, new Jerusalem, coming down from God out of heaven, prepared as a bride adorned for her husband." This is the consummation, the everlasting Joy of the Lamb; "the church of the firstborn, which is written in heaven"; "the Bride, the Lamb's Wife," in her final completeness and eternal abode, descending in her purity and beauty—the crowning gem in the heavenly diadem. The New Jerusalem is the realization of that celestial city which Christ has gone to prepare and to bring down from heaven, to be the eternal home of His Glorified Saints. The faithful of all ages have been inspired by the promise of a dwelling place of heavenly blessedness; an enduring city built and prepared by the Author and Finisher of our faith.

"These all died in faith . . . and confessed that they were strangers and pilgrims on the earth" (Hebrews 11:13). "[Abraham] looked for a city which hath foundations, whose builder and maker is God" (Hebrews 11:10). "[God] hath prepared for them a city" (Hebrews 11:16). "In my Father's house are many mansions. . . . I go to prepare a place for you . . ." (John 14:1–6).

Some protest the idea of a literal city, declaring the apocalyptic visions to be symbolic; but those Bible-lovers who are old-fashioned enough to believe with simple childlike faith that God means exactly what He says, in every generation, have been blessed and inspired with the heavenly hope of a real, literal, God-built, enduring and eternal *home*.

The city is called "the Bride, the Lamb's Wife." A city is a city only in the sense of those who inhabit it. Without residents a city would be an empty sepulcher. So it is that the heavenly city is the Lamb's Bride because of the ransomed, redeemed and glorified ones who dwell within its jasper walls. The streets of transparent gold; the many mansions, the crystal-clear river, the trees of everlasting fruitage, the beauty of accommodation and arrangement, together with its immortal occupants, make it both *a city* and *a people*—thus, did the angel describe it; " . . . the bride, the Lamb's wife . . . that great city, the holy Jerusalem . . ." (21:9–10).

"And the city had no need of the sun, neither of the moon, to shine in it: for the glory of God did lighten it, and the Lamb is the light thereof" (21:23).

THE HOLY OCCUPANTS.

"And I heard a great voice out of heaven saying, Behold, the tabernacle of God is with men [mankind], and he will dwell with them, and they shall be his people, and God himself shall be with them, and be their God" (21:3). The glorified saints are the dwellers of the celestial city, the Tabernacle of God. Yet John speaks of another company, "the nations of

THE FATE OF ECCLESIASTICAL BABYLON (17:1–18).

"And there came one of the seven angels which had the seven vials, and talked with me, saying unto me, Come hither; I will shew unto thee the judgment of the great whore that sitteth upon many waters . . ." (17:1–2). We have learned in previous chapters (14:8; 16–9) of Babylon and the calamity befalling her. The description of God's final dealings with Babylon are given in detail in chapter 17 and 18. The chapters reveal the final destruction of great Babylon in its ecclesiastical, political and commercial aspects. Chapter 17 first deals with Babylon as a great universal system representing false religion; it is called "the great whore" (Greek *porne*, harlot). It does not represent one religious institution, the Papacy, as some believe because of its purple and scarlet array, it is evidently the combined companies of apostate Protestantism, Romanism, the large and varied groups of false cults, rank modernism and even a sprinkle of atheism, **the great ecumenical religious monstrosity predicted of the last days** (1 Timothy 4:1).

The obvious foundation of this great ecumenical movement is now being laid before our eyes, and acclaimed as a great move toward tolerance, understanding and peace, while becoming more and more estranged from "the faith which was once delivered unto the saints" (Jude 3).

Her secularized alliances with the godless world-system is called *fornication,* the symbolism of spiritual adultery (James 4:4). Her harlotry is said to extend to *many waters,* that is, "peoples, and multitudes, and nations, and tongues" (17:15).

The Babylon of old was the center of idolatrous worship—a system inspired by Satan to distract from the worship of the true and living God. The system of Babylonian idolatry or spiritual fornication rapidly engulfed the nations, even contaminating God's elect. Whether viewed as a city or a religious system (she evidently is both) the Babylon of spiritual corruption is the culmination of a system of ecclesiastical harlotry by which the delusions of the false prophet, on behalf of the Antichrist, have intoxicated the nations with its sorceries (Revelation 13:11–15).

THE WOMAN ON THE BEAST (17:3–4).

" . . . I saw a woman sit upon a scarlet coloured beast, full of names of blasphemy, having seven heads and ten horns. And the woman was arrayed in purple and scarlet colour, and decked with gold and precious stones and pearls, having a golden cup in her hand full of abominations and filthiness of her fornication."

John sees the woman (ecclesiastical Babylon) named the harlot for her illicit intercourse with the godless world-system, sitting upon a scarlet colored beast—the great political world power. The angel explains the mystery. "And upon her forehead was a name written, MYSTERY, BABYLON THE GREAT, THE MOTHER OF HARLOTS AND ABOMINATIONS OF THE EARTH" (17:5).

The study of Babylon is a lengthy and revealing subject. Much is written concerning Babylon throughout the Scriptures, beginning with the reference to Babel in Genesis 10:8–10. As space will not permit a lengthy study, a brief review of the Babylon of old and the prophetic vision of Babylon of the last days consummated in chapters 17 and 18 will help us, in a measure, to better understand the revelation before us. (*The Two Babylons* by Rev. Alexander Hislop, is a remarkable and fully documented work on the subject.)

"And upon her forehead was a name written, MYSTERY . . . ." In this instance Mystery Babylon is not a reference to Babylon as a city but to the pseudo religious aspect of her full name, Mother of Harlots. The word mystery is not an adjective but part of a descriptive title. Not mysterious but something which has hitherto been hidden and is now exposed, as the abominable pagan superstitions, rites and unscriptural practices that form an essential part of the corrupt ecclesiastical system. Church history reveals the pagan features of the mystery religion of Babylon being gradually absorbed into the Christian faith until they became intolerable to many leaders in the Roman Church who uttered their voices in protest and came out from among them in the Great Reformation of the sixteenth century.

Babylon of old was the center of early civilization. Having forsaken the recognition of the one true and living God of their patriarchal forefather Noah—like the Egyptians, the descendants of Mizraim (grandson of Noah)—they invented a system of religious practises and multiple gods of their own. Nimrod was probably the architect of the great Tower of Babel and the Satan-inspired conspiracy to centralize the power and influence of a one-world system, which would rule God out of the affairs of man and destroy the purpose and hope of inner, spiritual unity of a world centered in God.

"Let us," "Let us" was the rallying slogan of the satanic scheme (Genesis 11:1–9). **This was man's first attempt at a one-world political system and a religion without God.**

The scheme was confounded by God, but nevertheless Satan, the instigator, has never given up the presumptuous conspiracy. Now, in the vision of the last days of world affairs, we recognize the fulfillment of Satan's age-long ambition—**one world and one church formed and dominated by the Satanic trinity.** But, thanks be to God, it is again confounded and, this time, brought to total and everlasting destruction by the return of earth's rightful Lord and King with power and with great glory (Matthew 24:30).

As the true church, the Bride of Christ is called a mystery hid from other ages (Ephesians 3:3–6), so this woman whose name was Mystery, the Mother of Harlots, is Satan's counterfeit.

Referring back to 17:3, " . . . I saw a woman sit upon a scarlet colored beast . . . having seven heads and ten horns;" verse 8 of the same chapter reveals both where he came from and where he is going—" . . . shall ascend out of the bottomless pit, and shall go into perdition." The seven heads of the beast are first said to be "seven mountains, on which the woman sitteth." The seven-hilled city is a common term in the history of Rome; thus, the significance of this revelation is geographical. "And there are seven kings . . . "—here the significance is, seemingly, personalized. Of these kings "Five are fallen, and one is, and the other is not yet come; and when he cometh, he must continue a short space" (verse 10).

It is interesting to note that, in John's lifetime, Rome ruled the then known world. There is no doubt that these kings mentioned are associated in some form of Rome's political rule. Some view them as representative of seven successive forms of government from the rise of the Roman Empire (the fourth world empire of Nebuchadnezzar's vision, Daniel 2:40–43), the established republic, the tribune, the senate, the triumvirates, and so on, to final and absolute dictatorship and emperor deification. Others view the kings as individual emperors, one of whom it is said "is" or existing at the time of John's writing. Of the seven kings that verse 10 records, "five are fallen, one is [in John's day], and the other is not yet come . . . ."

It is clear, whatever the count, according to the panorama of future events as seen by John, that *the other* yet to come is spoken of definitely as a person: "When he cometh, he must continue a short space." By following the relative references in the apocalyptic visions that this person is the Antichrist there is no question that he is the last world ruler and that his reign or *continuing* is a short space or duration. And it is his fate that is declared; he "goeth into perdition" (17:10–11), confirmed in chapter 19:20.

"And the ten horns which thou sawest are ten kings, which have received no kingdom as yet, but receive power as kings one hour with the beast. These have one mind, and shall give their power [Greek *exousia,* authority] and strength unto the beast." For many years students of prophecy have spoken much of the revival of the ancient Roman Empire in a form predicted in the prophecies of Daniel—in which the rise, course and final stage or form of the old Roman governmental system is defined as having "ten horns" (Daniel 7:7)—"and the ten horns out of this kingdom are ten kings that shall arise . . ." (Daniel 7:24).

Nearing the end of the revelation John beheld the last form of gentile world power as a confederacy of ten kingdoms. The kings, the angel revealed, have no kingdoms as yet, but receive authority as kings at the end time. They receive this authority with the beast. In other words, the beast and the ten horns or powers are contemporary. They place themselves, however, in subjection to him. The Greek text reads "These have one mind, and the power (*dunamis*) and authority (*exousia*) of themselves to the beast they shall give up." In chapter 13:7–8 we read that " . . . power (*exousia*) was given him over all kindreds, and tongues, and nations. And all that dwell upon the earth shall worship him."

"These shall make war with the Lamb, and the Lamb shall overcome them: for he is Lord of lords, and King of kings . . . " (17:14). This is the last mad blasphemous act of the Antichrist and his allies. The battle is described in chapter 19:19–21. The conflict had not yet begun but the angel announces the victory with certain anticipation.

"And the ten horns which thou sawest upon the beast (a better reading is they [the horns] and the beast) these shall hate the whore, and shall make

heal, for the tormented ones are still blaspheming God because of their suffering after the fifth bowl has been outpoured (16:11).

THE SECOND VIAL (16:3).

"The second angel poured out his vial upon the sea; and it became as the blood of a dead man: and every living soul died in the sea." It will be remembered that at the sounding of the second trumpet, one third part of the sea became blood, and a third part of the sea creatures died. Now, with the outpouring of the second bowl the judgment is complete; all the sea is contaminated so that all the remaining creatures die. Should the word here defined as *sea* mean "the continuous body of saline water that covers 70.8 percent of the exterior of the earth's surface, to an average depth of 12,500 feet, and a maximum depth of 35,800 feet" (according to the encyclopedia), it staggers the imagination to try to visualize the billions of floating, rotting shoals of dead and dying sea creatures, and the awful unbearable stench, the harbinger of disease, in such a tremendous body of the earth's surface like unto the congealing blood of one dead.

THE THIRD VIAL (16:4–7).

"And the third angel poured out his vial upon the rivers and fountains of waters; and they became blood." With the outpouring of the contents of the third bowl, the wrath of God follows the pattern of the third trumpet judgment which fell upon the third part of the rivers and fountains of water —the earth's fresh water system and the sustainer of life—for thirst is more terrifying than hunger. We look upon the beauty of the cascading waters, all of the springs sparkling in the sunlight as they feed the mighty rivers and fountains of the earth, but in the day of God's visitation these mighty life-sustaining waters, as John saw them in prophetic vision *became* (Greek *egeneto*) blood. There is no *as* or *like unto* in this day of judgment. God's judgments are just. The blood of the saints and the prophets was literal blood indeed. God, the righteous judge, is judging those who shed the blood of saints in kind—blood shall be their drink. The prayers of the slaughtered martyrs for divine vengeance must be finally and fully answered. To turn the other cheek when men shall smite thee was Christ's embodiment of Grace, but this is judgment. The pleading voice of grace and mercy are now silenced by the thunders of Divine wrath. "And [writes John] I heard another out of the altar say, Even so, Lord God Almighty, true and righteous are thy judgments" (16:7).

THE FOURTH VIAL (16:8–9).

"And the fourth angel poured out his vial upon the sun; and power was given unto him [the sun] to scorch men with fire." The fourth trumpet judgment had to do with the celestial bodies—the sun, moon and stars—both the light of day and night was darkened by one third of its light. The fourth vial apparently affected the sun alone; the intensity of its heat was increased until it scorched men with its fire. And rather than repent men "blasphemed the name of God, which hath power over these plagues." They knew full well it was the hand of divine judgment, and yet "they repented not to give him glory."

THE FIFTH VIAL (16:10–11).

"And the fifth angel poured out his vial upon the seat [Greek *thronos*, throne] of the beast; and his kingdom was full of darkness; and they gnawed their tongues for pain." The fifth bowl to be poured out by the fifth angel is directed at the very source of the world's wickedness, namely, the throne of the beast (the Antichrist), the seat of satanic power and authority. The result of the judgment was darkness filling his kingdom. Although Satan's kingdom is a kingdom of darkness, this judgment was undoubtedly like unto the thick darkness that covered Egypt in the day of God's outpoured plagues, described as "even darkness which may be felt . . . . They saw not one another" (Exodus 10:21-23), making the Antichrist's blasphemous operations difficult to the point of the impossible. Adding to people's misery and confusion was the continuing pains from the loathsome sores of the previous judgment until "they gnawed their tongues [the yielded instruments of their blasphemies] . . . and repented not.

THE SIXTH VIAL (16:12–16).

"And the sixth angel poured out his vial upon the great river Euphrates; and the water thereof was dried up, that the way of the kings of the east might be prepared." The outpouring of the sixth bowl of wrath is directed upon the River Euphrates. That this action upon the great river, as seen in the prophetic panorama by John, was actual and literal, we have no reason to doubt when we consider the source from which the judgments of the Apocalypse came—namely the hand of Almighty God. For, as the angel Gabriel gave Mary the assurance that "with God nothing shall be impossible" (Luke 1:37), surely we too have the divine assurance that God means exactly what He says in His own time and in His own divine and eternal purpose.

God even condescends to explain His purpose in drying up the river; "that the way of the kings of the east [literally sun-rising] might be prepared" (16:12). When we read of the events to follow under the outpouring of the same (sixth) vial, we learn that the kings of the whole world are preparing to gather "to the battle of the great day of God Almighty" (16:14). The drying up of the great river (a broad barrier to marching armies) was to facilitate the crossing of the rulers from the east and their armies in their mad march to join forces from all over the world to the final battle of Armageddon.

John continues with the description of the scene; "And I saw three unclean spirits like frogs come out of the mouth of the dragon, and . . . the false prophet. For they are the spirits of devils" (Greek *daimonon*, demons) There is only one Devil (Greek *diabolos*).

CHART NO. 11

Not only is the great river dried up on the outpouring of the sixth bowl, but the action also invokes demon spirits—controlled by the Satanic trinity—to deceive and lure the nations to their doom. In the 16th verse, we read, "And he [God] gathered them [the armies of the world under the Antichrist] together into a place called in the Hebrew tongue Armageddon." It is God Almighty, in righteous retribution, who gathers them to this place of judicial judgment, employing the very satanic trinity itself to carry out the divine purpose. It has been well said, "The Dragon is anti-God, the Beast anti-Christ, the False Prophet anti-Spirit, a trinity of Hell."

A warning admonition before the last bowl. In the midst of this prophetic rehearsal, as it were, concerning the coming battle of Armageddon and its subsequent results—the last bowl judgment—there is a solemn pause while our Lord Himself speaks with loving concern to those who have thus far faithfully endured the snares of the Antichrist and the Devil-inspired allurements around about them. "Behold, I come as a thief. Blessed is he that watcheth, and keepeth his garments, lest he walk naked, and they see his shame" (16:15). "As a thief," this is Christ's coming to the world. Although forewarned, the exact time of His coming is unannounced and will catch the world in a snare of darkness and delusion. Here we see the gracious assurance of Paul's words to the ready, waiting and watching ones of the true Church "But ye, brethren, are not in darkness, that that day should overtake you as a thief [for] ye are all the children of light . . . " (1 Thessalonians 5:1-11).

THE SEVENTH VIAL (16:17–21).

"And the seventh angel poured out his vial into the air; and there came a great voice out of the temple of heaven, from the throne, saying, It is done." The outpoured contents of the seventh bowl was not directed to one certain location on earth, but into the air—the atmosphere surrounding the whole earth, thus the result of the outpouring was a world-wide catastrophic disturbance. Voices, thunders, lightnings, the most violent earthquake in the history of man that tumbled down cities and swallowed up the islands and mountains—all of this terror was accompanied by a great storm of hailstones about the weight of a talent (approximately 100 pounds). All that man had built, without God, in the name of temporal progress had collapsed.

Babylon appears to be a special object of God's wrath. Whether, as many believe, the reference is to Rome, which is understood by many expositors to be spiritual Babylon, or to the literal rebuilt city of Babylon on the Euphrates, God remembered amid the chaos "to give unto her the cup of the wine of the fierceness of his wrath" (16:19). The detailed fate of ecclesiastical Babylon forms the subject of the next two chapters (17–18).

The voice from the throne in heaven declares, **"It is done."** With all the pain, terror and multiplied sufferings of the blinded, deluded, arrogant, rebellious survivors of the awful and final judgments of God with hardened hearts they still blasphemed His name rather than repenting and throwing themselves upon His mercy hoping against hope that the gate of grace was not forever closed.

of the ages] before the Holy Angels who witnessed God's Christ tasting "death for every man." The same angels by whom the entire earthly mission and passion of our Saviour was seen (1 Timothy 3:16), now witness with Holy approval the everlasting punishment of those who turn their backs upon the Creator-Saviour to bow in world-wide acceptance and worship of the creature. This is hell-fire and brimstone preaching (proclaiming) poured out without mixture or compromise (14:10–11)—preaching that is ridiculed and resented in this our day of growing coldness, apathy and downright disregard of spiritual values. This is also preaching that is merciful in that judgment does not fall without every effort that heaven can make to warn the unrepentant world of the inevitable judgment. **The Fifth Vision** (14:13). "And I heard a voice from heaven saying unto me, Write, Blessed are the dead which die in the Lord from henceforth: Yea, saith the Spirit, that they may rest from their labours; and their works do follow them." "Here is the patience [endurance] of the saints, here are they that keep the commandments of God, and the faith of Jesus" (14:12).

During the great tribulation it is evident that many will refuse to bow and worship the Antichrist; faithfully keeping the commandment "Thou shalt not make unto thee any graven image . . . thou shalt not bow down thyself to them, nor serve them . . ." (Exodus 20:3–5). They are called blessed, and their works, standing true to their testimony, shall follow them (be recorded of them) in heaven. This is true not only of the tribulation saints but of all who die in the Lord.

The Sixth Vision is the angel with the sickle (14:14–16). "And I looked, and beheld a white cloud, and upon the cloud one sat like unto the Son of man, having on his head a golden crown, and in his hand a sharp sickle . . . ." In the vision of the harvest and later the vintage (14:17–20), we come face to face with the last administration of God's wrath, and angels are again viewed in their roles as executors in the exercise of judgment. The announced judgment upon the beast worshippers (14:9–11), and the time of reaping (the fulfillment of the judgment) is said to *have come*. The result is viewed as instantaneous, "and the earth was reaped."

This scene must not be confused with the Great White Throne judgment, the subjects of which are the resurrected, wicked dead (20:11–15). This is a premillennial judgment upon the rebellious Christ-rejecting earth dwellers. Those rejecting the truth and believing the lie (2 Thessalonians 2:8–12).

It would also appear that the harvest referred to, so closely connected with the vintage (the wine press of God's wrath), is most conclusively a harvest of Judgment. There is a harvest of evil as well as good (Luke 3:17). There is no note of joy at this reaping. In the continuity of events taking place at *the end of the age*, the harvest of the good seed has already been reaped in advance of the judgment scenes before us. The Rapture of the Church of the Firstborn is, most assuredly, the gathering of the wheat to the harvest home. The tares are "the children of the wicked one," and remain to their judgment and everlasting destruction—" . . . the harvest is the end of the world [age]; and the reapers are the angels" (Matthew 13:36–43).

The scene witnessed by John might well be a prophetic preview of Armageddon as seen by the prophet Joel (3:9–13). Particularly verse 13: "Put ye in the sickle, for the harvest is ripe . . . for their wickedness is great."

The Seventh Vision (14:17–20). "And another angel came out of the temple which is in heaven, he also having a sharp sickle. And another angel came out from the altar, which had power over fire; and cried . . . to him that had the sharp sickle, saying, Thrust in they sharp sickle, and gather the clusters of the vine of the earth; for her grapes are fully ripe. And the angel thrust in his sickle into the earth, and gathered the vine of the earth, and cast it into the great winepress of the wrath of God. And the winepress was trodden without the city, and blood came out . . . even unto the horses bridles, by a space of a thousand and six hundred furlongs" (200 miles).

The angel having power over fire comes forth from the brazen altar, the altar of judgment, commanding the angel out of the temple to "gather the clusters of the vine of the earth," as opposed to the true vine and its branches—Christ and His own (John 15:5).

The winepress being trodden "without the city," again may be in reference to Armageddon, which will be fought in the valley of Megiddo. So great will be the slaughter that blood will flow from the winepress, and in the description of the aftermath, all the fowls of the air will be filled with the flesh of the slain (19:18).

THE SEVEN LAST PLAGUES—THE VIAL JUDGMENTS (15:1 to 16:21).

"And I saw another sign in heaven, great and marvelous, seven angels having the seven last plagues; for in them is filled up the wrath of God" (15:1). The cup of iniquity is full with Satan's last blasphemous claim to divine worship and the kingship of the world, so also is the cup of the wrath of God "filled up." The time has come when the long-suffering patience towards the adamant rejection of mercy is exhausted, and the defiant earth-dwellers must drink of the wrath. "And I saw as it were a sea of glass mingled with fire: and them that had gotten the victory over the beast . . . ."

Earlier in the prophetic panorama John saw "a sea of glass like unto crystal" (4:6). In the vision before us it is "mingled with fire," for the whole prophetic scene to follow bespeaks judgment. Standing on the sea, as of glass, is that triumphant company who refused to worship the beast or receive his mark. They *overcame* by no strength of their own but "by the blood of the Lamb, and the word of their testimony; [for] they loved not their lives unto death" (12:11). "And they sing the song of Moses . . . and the Lamb . . ." (15:5–3).

PREPARATION FOR THE VIAL JUDGMENTS (15:5–8).

John beholds the scene in heaven. ". . . the temple of the tabernacle of the testimony in heaven was opened" (15:5). With our limited vision, for now we see through a glass darkly, it is difficult to visualize the glory of the Temple of God in heaven—the holy of holies, God's dwelling place, where He is worshiped and adored by the great celestial host and, in the scene before us, from which issue forth His righteous judgments. The earthly tabernacle with its furnishings, as sacred as they were to God's earthly people, were but copies of the things in heaven. (Hebrews 8:5).

In an earlier chapter the temple was opened, and here was seen the ark of the covenant and a golden altar which is associated with the covenanted promises of Jehovah toward Israel. These scenes were accompanied by thunders, lightnings and earthquake, but now from the temple, the curtains of the sanctuary being opened in the vision before us, seven angels came forth clothed in pure and white linen and having their breasts girded with golden girdles (15:5–6). And one of the living creatures spoken of as "in the midst of the throne" (4:6) "gave unto the seven angels seven golden vials full of the wrath of God . . ." The word *vial* (Greek *phiale*) suggests an open bowl.

As the seven angels received the command to "Go your ways" at the same time, it suggests an undelayed and quick succession of outpourings (16:1). "And the temple was filled with smoke from the glory and power of God." (15:7–8). Viewing the earthly scene Israel, God's covenanted people, is seen in covenant with the Antichrist (Daniel 9:27) and the nations paying homage to the Devil, the cup of God's wrath (Greek *thumos*, literally anger) is full. Smoke filled the temple so that none was able to enter until the judgment plagues were completed (15:8). No approach to God by man or angel, prayer or supplication could halt the outpouring of the long-suffering wrath of Almighty God. Reminding us of words of the Psalmist " . . . who may stand in thy sight when once thou are angry?" (Psalm 76:7).

In the unfolding panorama of prophetic events, each marks the nearness of Christ's coming to receive the rightful kingship of the world. There are three great signs that John beholds, around which all subsequent events associated with characters, companies, rejoicings and judgments mentioned in the entire revelation, whether direct or parenthetical, revolve: (1) the sign of the woman, Israel; (2) the sign of the great red dragon, the Devil, and the final world-system controlled by him and his emissaries; (3) the sign in heaven of seven angels having the seven last plagues of judgment upon a God-defying, Christ-rejecting world (*cosmos*).

CHART NO. 10

THE FIRST VIAL (Chapter 16).

"And the first went, and poured out his vial upon the earth; and there fell a noisome and grievous sore upon the men which had the mark of the beast, and upon them which worshiped his image" (16:2). The judgment poured out from the bowl of the first angel is directed upon a specifically singled out company. Those who had accepted the mark of the beast (the Antichrist), and were worshiping his image. The judgment, or plague is described as a grievous sore; evidently intensely painful boils that refused to

After the turbulent cycle of time the world is back where it was in the darkest days of the beginning, the scene of God's wrath against demonism, necromancy and all of the abominations of old. Now, the blasphemous climax is not only demonism but worship of the very Devil himself, in and through the man of sin, the Antichrist, who also receives the homage of the deluded world. Surely the cup of iniquity is full. For no man's life can be sustained unless he bows to the Devil and receives the mark or the number of the name of the Antichrist. The number of which is the number of a man—666.

There have been so many conjectures as to the meaning of these mystic numbers throughout this present dispensation, and as John writes, "Let him that hath understanding count the number." There is no doubt that after the Rapture of the Church, and that Wicked [one] is revealed (2 Thessalonians 2:6-12), there will be no mistake as to who this sinister world power will be and the significance of the number of his name. To the born-again believer it matters little, for our only confrontation with this emissary of Satan will be at his destruction (Revelation 19:20).

THE VISION OF THE LAMB and THE HARVEST OF GOD'S WRATH (Chapter 14).

Chapter 12 deals primarily with Israel and chapter 13 with the activity of the Satanic trinity. In chapter 14 we are assured of the triumph of the Lamb and the judgment of the wicked. The chapter consists of seven separate visions, not chronologically arranged, but each complete in itself, yet definitely related to the whole.

THE 144,000 WITH THE LAMB. (14:1-5)

"And I looked, and lo, the Lamb stood on the mount Sion, and with him an hundred and forty and four thousand, having his Father's name written in their foreheads." Many learned expositors are in agreement that the 144,000 of chapter 14 is the same company seen in chapter 7. "The [bondmen] servants of our God,"—the 144,000 of the twelve tribes of Israel, whom the angels sealed against injury and hurt in 7:2-8, are here standing triumphantly with the Lamb. Throughout the great tribulation period, they do not suffer martyrdom having been kept safely as God's witnesses throughout the Antichrist's blasphemous reign. Thus, in all evidence, this is an earthly scene.

In chapter 13 the worshipers of the Devil are identified by the mark of the beast on their hand and forehead. In chapter 14 those witnessing of God are identified by the Divine seal—the name of the Father written on their foreheads, marking their loyalty to the Lamb.

These are standing, prophetically in the vision, with the Lamb, having been sealed and kept by divine preservation to follow the Lamb whithersoever He goeth, as He joins them at His Second Coming, when His feet shall touch the Mount of Olives at the beginning of His Millennial Reign (Zechariah 14:4). Thus, viewing "the mount of Sion," in this scene, as the heavenly Jerusalem involves problems.

Speaking prophetically through the psalmist, the Father, addressing the raging and hostile Kings and rulers of the earth, declared, "Yet have I set my king upon my holy hill of Zion" (Psalm 2:6). This is prophetic forecast of earth's rightful King standing upon "the mount Sion" (Revelation 14:1); the earthly Jerusalem from whence He shall reign gloriously. And standing triumphantly with Him are the 144,000 sealed "servants of our God." For He shall not only be "glorified in his saints" at His coming, but also "to be admired in all them that believe . . . in that day" (2 Thessalonians 1:10). Thus, this particular *sealed* company, spoken of as "the servants of our God" (7:1-8), are providentially kept and ready to enter into the Millennial blessedness as the "first fruits" of the nation of Israel, restored, redeemed and protected, and to form the nucleus of the living nation of Israel in its place of prominence in the Millennial Kingdom. (Zechariah 8:22-23). Standing with the Lamb, they are the connecting link of the dispensations. They sang the song of redemption (14:2-3). Their song was, as it were, a new song. John had heard the song of the redeemed "out of every kindred, and tongue, and people, and nation," a great heavenly choir with the angel hosts adding their voices of praise and adoration (5:9-10). This song, however, was one which "no man could learn" save the 144,000 sealed and redeemed of Israel. "And I heard the voice of harpers harping upon their harps." This scene is beautifully logical, for throughout Israel's turbulent history, the harp is mentioned so often on occasions associated with joy. During the captivity, we read "By the rivers of Babylon . . . we wept . . . and hanged our harps upon the willows"—their song had ceased. But now, with the sorrows of the great tribulation past, standing with their Messiah-King, they shall take up their harps and sing a new redemption song to the everlasting Glory of Jehovah.

There is another announcement regarding the 144,000 whom John describes as *virgins*. Some interpret this difficult description as abstinence from marriage during the abnormal days and trying circumstances of the tribulation; others take the view described in Grimm's Greek Lexicon as "one who has abstained from all uncleanness and whoredom attendant to idolatry." In this case, not defiled by the prevailing influence of the great whore (17:1-2) and keeping themselves free from spiritual fornication amidst an adulterous world-system. The following verse seems to give credence to the latter thought—"These are they which follow the Lamb whithersoever he goeth." A truly separated and sanctified company ready to follow the Lamb as He stands on mount Sion, the earthly Jerusalem, which will be the capital of the Millennial Kingdom. Thus, the first of the seven visions of chapter 14 is the vision of the Lamb and the 144,000. **The Second Vision** (14:6-7). "And I saw another angel fly in the midst of heaven, having . . . everlasting gospel" (no article) to proclaim to the whole world. There is nothing whatsoever in the announcement about Grace or Redemption. The angel is not proclaiming the gospel of grace or the gospel of the Kingdom but the ageless gospel of God's sovereignty. It is a final and awesome reminder. Since the unrepentant, blinded world failed to respond to the plea of mercy, God, through His last company of earthly witnesses, reminds "them that dwell on the earth," that the hour of God's judgment has come. This is God's last call to an apostate world to recognize His sovereignty and to fear and worship Him as the Creator and Sustainer of all things (14:6-7; Psalm 2:10-12). **The Third Vision** (14:8) is the fall and doom of Babylon. "There followed another angel, saying Babylon is fallen, . . . that great city, because she made all nations drink of the wine of the wrath of her fornication." This verse is the prophetic pronouncement in brief of the fall of great Babylon; the details of its fulfillment are recorded in later chapters.

Babylon of old was the center of idolatrous worship; a system inspired by Satan to distract from and destroy the knowledge and worship of the true and living God. The system of Babylonian idolatry, or spiritual fornication, rapidly engulfed the nations even contaminating the worship of God's elect. Whether viewed as a city or a religious system, the Babylon of spiritual adultery and corruption is the culmination of a great system of ecclesiastical harlotry by which the delusions of the false prophet, on behalf of the Antichrist, have intoxicated nations with her sorceries (13:15).

The angel is heard crying, "Babylon is fallen, is fallen," in anticipation of judgment accomplished. The particulars of her destruction and its effect upon apostate Christendom and the corrupted nations are clearly revealed in chapters 17 and 18. Revelation 19:1-6 records the celebration in heaven; the great harlot is judged (19:2), and the true Bride shall soon be revealed (19:7-8). **The Fourth Vision** is the doom of the beast (Antichrist) worshipers. "And the third angel followed them, saying with a loud voice, If any man worship the beast and his image, and receive his mark in his forehead, or in his hand, The same shall drink of wine of the wrath of God, which is poured out without mixture into the cup of his indignation; and he shall be tormented with fire and brimstone in the presence of the holy angels, and in the presence of the Lamb."

In reviewing the detailed account of the previous announcement of the fall of Babylon, it is clear that the great political power, the consolidated empire of the Antichrist (17:12-13), turns and destroys the adulterous ecclesiastical system, the great harlot who was at first carried or supported by the world powers in return for her patronizing favors.

This leaves the Antichrist the sole possessor of world-wide power and authority. The mask of beneficence is dropped and the full development of evil is culminated by a relentless decree that all, rich and poor, great and small, must worship the beast and his image and receive the mark of absolute subjection on the penalty of death for refusal (13:15-18). Immediately an angel is dispatched from heaven announcing, that all might hear, the doom of those who obey the blasphemous edict. Receiving *the mark* of identification is an open testimony of the total acceptance of Satan's counterfeit Christ.

In the angel's warning there is no breath of mercy; it is the wine of God's wrath and "the smoke of their torment ascendeth for ever and ever" [for ages

devil, has been fighting and scheming to thwart God's plan of redemption ever since His (God's) first declaration, the germ of all Bible prophecy, recorded in Genesis 3:15. After the deception of Eve by Satan, God declared His intention to intervene. "I will put enmity between thee [Satan] and the woman, and between thy seed and her seed; it [her seed] shall bruise thy head, and thou shalt bruise his heel."

The enmity, however, was not confined to the serpent and the woman in the garden, but a God-declared state of perpetual conflict would exist throughout the generations of their respective seed. In verse 4 the dragon is seen standing before the travailing woman, waiting to devour her child. This takes us back to the events surrounding our Saviour's birth, and one specific incident of Satan's determination to destroy him. Matthew 2:13-18 records, for instance, the slaughter of the innocents.

The fifth verse (chapter 12) is a divine record of Satan's failure to destroy the Man Child, for He is "caught up unto God, and to his throne," where "He is able to save them to the uttermost that come unto God by him, seeing he ever liveth to make intercession for them" (Hebrews 7:25). Failing to destroy "the man child," Satan turns his wrath upon the woman, [Israel], "of whom as concerning the flesh Christ came . . ." (Romans 9:5) and the remnant of her seed (12:17).

There is, obviously, a tremendous interval of time between chapter 12:5, 6, which is not unusual in the study of Bible prophecy. Here, the present age of grace is not seen. The present prophetic gap begins in verse 5 with our Lord's ascension—being "caught up unto God"—and runs its course until the yet future days of the great tribulation, when the woman clearly identified as Israel flees from the persecution and wrath of Satan.

"And to the woman were given two wings of a great eagle, that she might fly into the wilderness . . ." (symbolizing sure and speedy flight to a place of refuge prepared by God). There to be succored "for a time, and times, and half a time" (three-and-a-half years, or 1260 days) 12:13-17. Even as God reminded this people after their escape from the Egyptian bondage " . . . I bare you on eagles' wings, and brought you unto myself."

Prior to the woman's (Israel's) persecution and flight to the safety of the wilderness, verses 7 to 12

are extremely important, revealing the great conflict which occurred in the heavens (the aerial regions, Satan's realm of operation since being cast out of heaven).

WAR IN HEAVEN (12:7-12).

"And there was war in heaven: Michael and his angels fought against the dragon . . . and his angels." Here John's gaze is directed from the age-end scenes on earth once again to a scene above. This time the action takes place in the heavens, the stellar heavens which is now the abode of Satan and his angels. The realm in which he is referred to in Ephesians 2:2 as "the prince of the power [Greek *exousia*, authority] of the air."

Michael, the only named archangel in the Scriptures, who formerly dared not bring a railing accusation against Satan, now is given authority, power and leadership to marshall the Holy Angels to engage Satan and his angels in a determinate contest. Frustrated and desperate in beholding the dominion of death broken, in the resurrection of the saints and the living ones escaping death's embrace by being clothed upon with immortality (1 Corinthians 15:51-57; 1 Thessalonians 4:15-18), Satan musters to battle all of the principalities, powers and every demon at his command, rallying his forces to meet the next challenge to his blasphemous ego—the cleansing of the heavenly spheres of his foul presence forever. The victory of Michael and his army is the utter rout of Satan. The record reads: " . . . neither was their place found any more in heaven . . . he was cast out into the earth, and his angels were cast out with him" (12:8-9).

Verse 10 is a declaration of triumphant victory. The casting down of Satan and "the rulers of the darkness of this world" clears the way, as it were, for " . . . salvation, and strength, and the kingdom of our God, and the power (Greek *exousia*, authority) of his Christ." A glorious announcement of the coming Kingdom and earth's rightful King. There was great victory, but a great woe is predicted upon the inhabitants of the earth and sea. The devil having been cast down to the earth is filled with great wrath "because he knoweth that he hath but a short time" —three-and-one-half years, the time of unparalleled tribulation prophecied by Daniel (9:27) and by

our Lord (Matthew 24:21)—the same short time that those of Israel are divinely protected in the wilderness. History is a record of the fact that every power that has attempted to wipe out the Jew has been thwarted to their own destruction, from Haman of old to the Hitlers of our day.

THE BEAST AND HIS FALSE PROPHET
(chapter 13).

These characters who are central figures in the events of the great tribulation, are spoken of as beasts. These are not animal monstrosities, the metaphors are actually a description of world powers, having the characteristics of the animals portrayed. We use the same language in a sense, when we speak of the Russian bear, the Chinese dragon, the American eagle and so on. An example is seen in Daniel's visions, for instance; the swift conquests of Alexander of Greece symbolized by the agile swiftness of a leopard (Daniel 7:6).

We know that Satan is a spirit-being and can only operate effectively in the human sphere by embodying himself in an earthly organism—the mind and body of man. This he seeks to do continually with his demon hosts.

The prophecy before us reveals the activity of two such beasts (men activated by satanic power). The first arises "out of the sea" (generally regarded as the masses of the nations in their restless agitation). He has seven heads and ten horns, and on its horns ten crowns and upon his heads the name of blasphemy (13:5-6). In 11:7 it affirms that he came out of the bottomless pit, confirming his league with Satan.

The seven heads denote completeness of (delegated) wisdom; the ten horns represent confederated political power, the crowns authority to rule. With these qualifications he will represent just what the Christ-rejecting world is waiting for—a super-leader to solve the problems of all mankind which is open blasphemy against God and His Christ.

Satan, knowing that his time is short, gives his power (Greek *dunamis*), his throne (as god of this world) and authority (Greek *exousia*), to *the beast* (who is a man rising to world power from among the masses of desperately restless humanity).

There is no mistaking the identity of this coming, sinister world power; Revelation 13:1-10 is a description of his political sovereignty over the whole world (*cosmos—the world order*). His composite portrait is spread throughout the Scriptures, both Old and New. He is the beast of Revelation 11:7 and 13:1. He is the Horn, or world power, of Daniel 7:24-26, the Desolator of Daniel 9:27, "the abomination of desolation" of Matthew 24:15, the "King of fierce countenance" of Daniel 8:23-25 are among many references personifying the world's last tyrannical ruler, who is doomed to destruction when the cup of iniquity is full.

Brought from the pit (11:7) in some mysterious sense, this tool of Satan becomes the incarnation of his malignant master.

CHART NO. 9

"And I beheld another beast coming up out of the earth; and he had two horns like a lamb, and he spake like a dragon" (13:11). As the Holy Trinity is the embodiment of Godliness, so the embodiment of evil is manifested in a counterfeit trinity. One is **the Dragon**, that old serpent the Devil (Greek *diabolos*) 12:9. Two is the **Antichrist**, the blasphemous leader of the last Satan-inspired world-system (13:1-10). Three is the **False Prophet**, the third person of the evil trio, the culmination of all ecclesiastical heresies, who by his deceptive propaganda (lamblike in its appearance but fierce and unrelentingly cruel in its behests) will cause the whole world (the church having been taken out of the world) to worship the first beast and with the evil assistance of the false prophet, will set him up as God in the Temple of God (2 Thessalonians 2:1-13).

Of the false prophet it is written: "He maketh fire come down from heaven . . . in the sight of men." Among the signs and lying wonders he will cause an image of the first beast (the Antichrist) to be erected, having power to give breath (Greek *pneuma*) to the image and to cause it to speak and demand all to worship the image upon threat of death to the disobedient (13:11-18). With a master stroke of satanic strategy he will cause all, with no exception, to receive the visible identifying mark of the beast or be denied the very means of subsistence—to buy or sell the vital necessities of life (13:16-17).

"And they worshipped the Dragon [Satan] . . . and they worshipped the beast . . . " [the Antichrist].

the Antichrist, while the overthrow of Jewish worship and the treading underfoot of the city occurs in the last half of his diabolical reign.

THE TWO WITNESSES (11:3-12). "I will give power unto my two witnesses and they shall prophesy a thousand two hundred and threescore days [forty-two months or three-and-a-half years]."

There is much debate as to the identity of these two witnesses. Some believe them to be Elijah and Enoch, and to support their claim, they quote the rule of Hebrew 9:27, "It is appointed unto men once to die . . . ." Both Elijah and Enoch were translated to heaven without tasting death! But the claim is nullified in the fact that all of the living saints at the time of the Rapture will escape death, being clothed with immortality.

Others believe them to be Elijah and Moses, but as these two witnesses die (11:7) the question naturally arises, could Moses die a second time? And so the debate continues. In verse 10 they are divinely designated as "**these two prophets**," thus if God chooses to obscure their identity perhaps the most important interest is not in who they are, but what God purposes in and through them.

The fact that while witnessing "these two prophets" needed divine protection lest they be slain, would make it seem more likely that being God's last witnesses their fearless testimony was purposed of God for the very last days of opportunity for the deceived masses to seek the true and living God: "before the great and dreadful day of the Lord" (Malachi 4:5).

"These two witnesses" are described as the two olive trees, and the two candlesticks (lampstands). These figures, carried over from Zechariah 4:3-14, indicate that they are anointed ones—lightbearers—testifying of God's truth in the darkest days of human history. They are given judgment power for judgment days. No man or scheme can harm them until their testimony is finished. Only by God's permissive will can their persecutors silence them by death at the hands of the beast of the bottomless pit to whom the dragon (Satan) gave his power and authority (13:1-2).

Their death causes great jubilation, as their dead bodies are publicly displayed for three-and-a-half days. The rejoicing of the multitude, however, is but short lived for after the three-and-a-half days "the Spirit of life from God entered into them, and they stood upon their feet; and great fear fell upon them which saw them." Adding to their terror, they heard a great voice from heaven saying, "Come up hither," and to the utter amazement of the now fearful multitude, they actually saw the two prophets whom they had slain, now alive and ascending up to heaven in the cloud (the use of the definite article suggests *the* cloud—the Shekinah glory).

THE SECOND WOE (11:13-14). "And the same hour was there a great earthquake . . . ." As literal an earthquake as that which attended both the death and the resurrection of the Son of God. John beheld a tenth part of the city crumble, and the death toll was 7000. The survivors were terrified and "gave glory to the God of heaven"—not the glory however of salvation through repentance but fearful recognition of divine power.

In summing up the events which occurred during the interval which began after the sounding of the sixth trumpet and continued to the time of the testimony, death, resurrection and ascension of the two witnesses, in verse 14 it is declared that "The second woe is past; and, behold, the third woe cometh quickly."

THE SEVENTH TRUMPET (11:15-19). "And the seventh angel blew his trumpet. There arose loud voices in Heaven and they were saying, the kingship of the world now belongs to our Lord and to his Christ, and he shall be king for timeless ages!" (Phillips Translation).

The sounding of the seventh trumpet is the proclamation to the whole disturbed universe that Christ, as King of kings and Lord of lords, after overthrowing Satan the usurper and destroying forever his kingdom of darkness, will set up His own Kingdom of Righteousness and reign to the ages of ages. Released from the powers of darkness the whole earth shall be filled with His Glory.

Upon hearing the long awaited proclamation the four and twenty elders prostrate themselves and worship God for at last assuming His everlasting Kingship in the earth (11:17).

While there is rejoicing in heaven, there is a display of anger on earth. This is not surprising when the unrepentant realize their doom, while the prophets and the saints of God (whom they despised with satanic hate) are now to receive their reward (11:18).

"And the temple of God was opened in heaven," and the ark of His testament was seen, attended with lightnings, voices, thunderings, an earthquake, and great hail. The ark of His covenant was a reminder of His unchanging faithfulness toward His people Israel (Psalm 135:4) before the final outpouring of judgment.

The temple of God in heaven must be a literal, celestial temple for Moses was instructed to "See . . . that thou make all things according to [the earthly tabernacle and its furnishings] the pattern shewed unto thee in the mount." In Hebrews 9:23 they were called patterns (copies, or likenesses) of things in heaven. Originally the earthly tabernacle and earthly worship was patterned after the heavenly, but sin defiled the earthly. Therefore, when Christ laid down His life as the sacrificial Lamb, "the veil of the temple was rent in twain from the top to the bottom" (Matthew 27:51); the way into the holiest was opened, and the unapproachable became approachable for whosoever will. The opening of the temple in heaven (11:19) is the last display of assuring glory before the on-coming flood of judgment. The worship of both worlds is the answer to as it is in heaven so shall it be on earth.

THE WOMAN AND THE MAN CHILD (12:1-6).

The opening verses of chapter 12 reveal two wonders, literally signs. The first is called "a great wonder, the second "another wonder." The word for sign (Greek *semeion*) is used seven times in the Apocalypse, indicating an object of important revelation. The first sign is that of "a woman clothed with the sun."

We cannot read far, beginning with the last verse of chapter 11 (which, speaking of "the ark of his testament" is associated with Israel) through chapter 12 to 14, without realizing that the content leads prophetically to Israel: the land, the temple, the city, the final judgment called Jacob's trouble, the salvation of the Godly remnant, and many other characteristics associated with Israel's history, causing us to realize that these chapters form a parenthesis before the resumption of the outpouring of God's wrath as revealed in the vial (or bowl) judgments beginning with chapter 15.

Reviewing, from our present study chapter 12, the beginning of the parenthesis, "a woman clothed with the sun, and the moon under her feet, and upon her head a crown of twelve stars. And she being with child cried, travailing in birth . . . and she brought forth a man child, who was to rule all nations . . ." (12:1-2; 5).

It can only be said of Israel that she brought forth a man child who was to rule all nations with a rod of iron (Revelation 19:15), none other than the Lord Jesus Christ. The divine mission of Israel as the chosen vessel, a nation separated unto God, was to bring forth the promised Redeemer.

One of the most direct revelations are the words of the Prophet Isaiah, "The Lord himself shall give you [Israel] a sign: "Behold, a virgin shall conceive, and bear a son, and shall call his name Immanuel" (*God with us*) Isaiah 7:14; Matthew 1:23.

CHART NO. 8

THE SECOND WONDER, or sign, in chapter 12, is "a great red dragon" (verse 3). We have no difficulty identifying this sign, it is "that old serpent, called the Devil and Satan, which deceiveth the whole world . . ." (verse 9). In the description of Satan in these verses we realize the power and authority with which this deceptive usurper operates in this present world system. Our Lord refers to him as "the prince of this world" (*cosmos*).

John sees him, (verses 3 and 4), as having seven heads, with crowns upon them, and ten horns, identifying him immediately with the beast (the Antichrist of chapter 13:1) who derives his authority from Satan. As verse 9 identifies this symbolic dragon as Satan, it is not difficult to trace his career as Lucifer, of whom it is written that he was full [or completeness] of wisdom. (Ezekial 28:12-19), which is symbolized in 13:1 by seven heads and seven crowns. Heads when crowned imply political rulership—here, usurped authority. His tail, we read, drew one third part of the stars of heaven. These stars are not literal stars, for what John saw was a sign or symbol.

When God laid the foundation of the earth, we are told "the morning stars sang together" (Job 38:7), hence, we take it that these stars were celestial spectators, the angel hosts. Thus, we understand that a third part of the angelic hosts were infected by Lucifer's spirit of revolt, and he drew them with him, as it were, in his own expulsion from heaven.

The dragon, identified as that old serpent the

Thus, in summarizing the judgment under the sound of the fifth trumpet blast, John is caused to write, "One woe is past; and behold, there come two woes more hereafter" (9:12).

THE SIXTH TRUMPET (9:13-21).

"And the sixth angel sounded [his trumpet], and I heard a voice from the four horns of the golden altar which is before God, Saying . . . Loose the four angels which are bound in the great river Euphrates."

The golden altar (the blood of the Levitical sacrifices was put on its golden horns) is referred to only twice in the visions, here and in chapter 8:3 where, evidently the same angel officiating as a priest now directed the sixth angel to loose the four angels bound at the Euphrates. "And the four angels were loosed, which were prepared for an hour, and a day, and a month, and a year, for to slay the third part of men. And the number of the army of the horsemen were two hundred thousand thousand."

These four angels of Satan's hierarchy were bound (and continue to be so according to the perfect tense)—prepared for this particular moment until God in His own time and purpose gave the command for them to be loosed.

The agents appointed to execute this ominous judgment (the slaughter of one third part of men) was a great army of two hundred million horsemen. Some expositors are reluctant to accept this number literally, for they contend it would mean the largest military force ever possible to assemble. However, when a specific number is given it can hardly be classified as innumerable. John said "I heard the number" (9:16) as though to confirm it.

The origin of this great army is not revealed and is more uncertain than the number. Its weapons are described as fire, smoke, and brimstone (elements of hell). If we take as literal the torment of the wicked with fire and brimstone (Revelation 14:10-11), and the lake of fire and brimstone (Revelation 20:10), the association of these hellish elements, together with the description of the horses and those that sat upon them, give the same impression as the description of the swarm of hellish locusts—that of a vast horde of demon-horsemen. Others find it not impossible to believe them to be a vast army of literal human horsemen armed with the most modern weapons, symbolized as flame, gasses and mechanical warfare. Whichever it may be it is representative of mass destruction of one third of the earth's remaining population.

Verse 20 speaks of "the rest of the men which were not killed." In the midst of the terrible woe, God stays the hand of slaughter for a demonstration, it would seem, of the utter wickedness of the rebellious heart of man. After such a visitation of wrath one would think men would cry out for mercy, yet the same verse reveals the awful truth that "Yet [they] repented not." Instead of repentance, sin will continue to abound, and "evil men . . . shall wax worse and worse." More than ever before men will turn to demon worship, idolatry, murder and violence. "The salt of the earth" with its restraining presence having been removed from the earthly scene, an utter collapse of all moral restraint will result in a deluge of shameless immorality which shall know no bounds of human depravity.

Following the sounding of the sixth trumpet according to our thinking, we would expect the seventh angel to sound the seventh trumpet with its attendant woe to follow in immediate continuity. But as it was between the sixth and seventh seal, the judgments were suspended in God's purpose while a company of witnesses were sealed against harm and destruction to be poured out upon the unrepentant and rebellious earth dwellers. So between the sounding of the sixth and seventh trumpet another interlude, or parenthesis as it were, is prophetically recorded from chapters 10:1 to 11:14, the longest interlude between judgments. These pauses in the continuity of events are not unconnected records but parts of the overall vision unfolded as sections of the great panorama. The trumpet judgments (the seventh, and last) are resumed after the interlude.

CHART NO. 7

THE MIGHTY ANGEL WITH THE LITTLE BOOK (10:1).

"And I saw another . . . angel come down from heaven, clothed with a cloud . . . . And he had in his hand a little book open; and he set his right foot upon the sea, and his left foot on the earth . . . ."

In verse one a celestial messenger is introduced who is described as "another mighty angel." In the context of the whole vision, angels are appointed to execute the divine will and purpose. This one is identified as "another mighty angel." The word *another* (Greek *allons*) means another of the same kind—one of the angel host related to the judgments —*another angel* distinguishing him from the angel preceding him.

In chapter 5:2, the same Greek word *ischuros* meaning *strong, mighty,* is used to describe the angel proclaiming "Who is worthy to open the book." Therefore, it is difficult to identify this mighty or strong angel as the Lord Jesus Christ as some believe. Another point is that the angel comes down from heaven (as do all holy angels) to plant one foot on the sea and one on the earth, but there is no evidence in the vision that the Lord Jesus will make a descent from heaven to earth during the great tribulation. He will not descend until the consummation when His feet shall touch the Mount of Olives (Zechariah 14:4).

That the mighty angel of 10:1, as a messenger with a special and official proclamation, is entrusted with great authority there is no doubt. He is described as being "clothed with a cloud: and a rainbow was upon his head, and his face was as it were the sun." Some say this could only mean the Lord Jesus, but of the angel announcing the doom of Babylon, it is said that "the earth was lightened with his glory" (18:1), yet no Bible scholar identifies him as the Lord Jesus.

That the angel has great authority, however, is evidenced by his placing one foot on the sea and the other on the earth. He confirms his proclamation by oath with his hand raised to heaven, but he does not swear by himself, for He who created all things is greater than the messenger. The purpose of God is to announce to the whole world (cosmos) "that there should be time no longer."

Although the Greek word *chronos*, time, is used, it cannot be interpreted that time will cease at this proclamation. A thousand years (the Millennial Age) must run its course before time ceases and eternity is again ushered in. It rather means that there should be no longer an interval of time, that is, there should be no delay (as noted in the margin of most Bibles). The reason is made plain in verse 7, because the mystery of God will be consummated when the seventh angel begins to sound the seventh trumpet.

The hour of final judgment is come when He shall avenge the cry of His elect, and by His Son vindicate all of His attributes that have been challenged by the adversary. He will then utterly destroy the usurper and his kingdom of darkness and establish His Kingdom of everlasting righteousness. Thus, the two great mysteries, the mystery of Godliness and the mystery of iniquity are brought to their inevitable conclusion—righteousness must triumph over evil.

In the hand of the angel which standeth upon the sea and land John beheld an open book which the voice from heaven commanded him [John] to take from the angel's hand. Upon approaching the angel and asking him for the book, the angel told him to "take it and eat it up," declaring it would be bitter to his stomach, though sweet as honey to his taste. John ate the little book and it proved to be just as the angel had declared (10:8-11).

That the book is the word of God is evident, for after eating it, that is, assimilating the revelation, John is told that he "must prophesy again before many peoples, and nations, and tongues, and kings." A command to which John was obedient, as recorded in the following chapters—even to the judgment of the Great White Throne—the doom and destiny of all whose names are not recorded in the book of life.

Sweet and bitter is the Word of God. Sweet to the believing soul, but what could be more bitter than the pronouncement of doom and damnation to the unregenerate, unbelieving heart?

THE TEMPLE, THE TWO WITNESSES, THE SECOND WOE, THE SEVENTH TRUMPET. (11:1-2).

This chapter is considered a difficult but important one. The language of verses 1 and 2, speaking of the temple of God, is definitely Jewish in character, looking forward in anticipation to the rebuilt temple in the holy city of Jerusalem. God's Temple in this present dispensation is His Church (1 Corinthians 6:19). We are assured by many passages of Scripture, particularly the detailed account found in Ezekiel chapters 40 to 48, that a temple will be built in Jerusalem with many worshipers, an order of priesthood, an altar and sacrifices. This, undoubtedly, will be the temple in which the Antichrist will appear in the midst of the prophetic week of seven years (Daniel 9:27), demanding to be worshiped, "shewing himself that he is God" (II Thessalonians 2:4). This is "the abomination of desolation" attested by our Lord (Matthew 24:15).

Thus, it appears, that the orderly Temple worship will occur during the first half of the reign of

throne, and before the Lamb, clothed with white robes, and palms in their hands; and cried with a loud voice, saying, Salvation to our God which sitteth upon the throne, and unto the Lamb."

Upon John's puzzled inquiry "whence came they?" he was told that this company came out of great tribulation having made their robes white in the blood of the Lamb.

This group differs distinctly from the Raptured church saints, who were kept **from** the great tribulation, these came **out** of the time of sorrows. The saints are crowned and enthroned round about the throne; these stand before the throne. The Raptured saints have harps and vials (containing the prayers of the saints 5:8); these have palms in their hands (symbolizing victory and praise). The church saints become kings and priests sharing the reign of the King of kings; these serve Him in some special service "day and night in his temple . . ." (7:13–17). It is suggested by some expositors that this great company, redeemed because of the blood, will serve in the Millennial Temple; for in the New Jerusalem there will be no Temple and no night there.

THE TRUMPET JUDGMENTS. (Chapter 8).

In pausing for a moment to review the overall end-time happenings, we first think of the two great events that overshadow all others. These are the Rapture of the saints to heaven and the return of the glorified Saints accompanying the conquering King to earth to share His Millennial reign. In between these two great events a series of judgments run their full course—the seals, the trumpets and the vials of God's wrath. The seals were first opened to reveal their successive order. After six seal judgments were executed there was a temporary suspension of judgment that God might accomplish an act of mercy by sealing and saving a great multitude. Although the Holy Spirit, now resident in the body of believers here on earth ("Know ye not that your body is the temple of the Holy Ghost" (Corinthians 6:19), will accompany the Church saints when they are translated to heaven (2 Thessalonians 2:7), He will still operate in the hearts of men as he did before his descent on the day of Pentecost. The first company of 144,000 were to perform a special service of witness for Him; the second company of untold numbers were saved and made secure because of the blood. Whatever may have been the particular testimony of this latter company we are not told. It was not because of their suffering in the great tribulation that they stand before the throne of God, for the shed blood of the Lamb is the only basis of salvation, and as they ascribe their salvation to our God and the Lamb, we know that their robes could alone be made white by token of the blood.

After the suspension of judgment in God's mercy and purpose, Christ, the Lamb, is to resume the opening of the seals. "And when he had opened the seventh seal, there was silence in heaven about the space of half an hour." Upon the opening of the seventh and last seal there was a brief but ominous silence, as though all creation was holding its breath in anticipation of the terrifying onslaught of judgment to come.

In the awesome silence **John beheld seven angels and to them was given seven trumpets.** The seven angels to sound seven successive trumpet blasts proclaiming the final judgments to fall upon the wicked of the earth.

CHART NO. 6

THE FIRST TRUMPET (8:7) sounded and there followed hail and fire mingled with blood cast to the earth, burning one third of the trees and all of the grass, leaving a scene of stark desolation. Those who take the view that the hail, fire, blood, trees and grass are symbols would do well to remember the plagues outpoured on Egypt (Exodus 9:25) which is surely literal history.

THE SECOND TRUMPET (8:8–9). Upon the trumpet blast by the second angel, a great mountain, as it were, burning with fire was cast into the sea. The third part of the sea became blood causing the death of the third part of all living creatures in the sea, and the destruction of the third part of the world's shipping. When symbols are used in Bible language it is usually made plain, such as here, a great mountain *as it were.* Evidently the great burning mass (probably meteoric) looked like a great mountain ablaze to John as he recorded the scene. Concerning the waters it does not say *as it were,* hence we take it that the sea was literally turned to blood (as in Egypt's judgments, Exodus 7:19–21), and the third part of life in the sea died.

THE THIRD TRUMPET (8:10–11). "And there fell a great star from heaven, burning as it were a lamp, and it fell upon the third part of the rivers, and upon the fountains of waters"—the fresh-water system of the earth. "The name of the star is called Wormwood . . . and many men died of the waters, because they were made bitter." We speak of *falling stars* which are actually meteoric phenomenon. This star plunging into earth's great river system turned the waters into lethal bitterness.

THE FOURTH TRUMPET (8:12–13). The sounding of the fourth trumpet confirmed the prediction spoken by Christ in the Olivet discourse (Luke 21: 25–28) as a sign marking the nearness of His returning. As John beheld the prophetic scene, the third part of the sun and the moon and the stars were smitten. Only God can make His creation do His bidding. "In the beginning" on the fourth day He set the heavenly bodies in their respective places. With the sound of the fourth trumpet judgment, He shall withdraw one third of their light, both by day and by night.

At this time, still under the sound of the reverberating trumpet blast, John beheld an angel flying in the midst of the darkened midheaven crying, "Woe, woe, woe, to the inhabiters of the earth," because of the previous trumpet judgments and "of the three angels, which are yet to sound!"

To those whose minds and hearts are set upon the things of earth, the angel is sent crying a warning, that as terrible as the first four trumpet judgments are, the sounding of the last three trumpets yet to follow will be more terrifying than any judgments thus far experienced. These are called the Woe judgments: causing men to seek death which will evade them and leaving them exposed to the full severity of the final judgment which marks the consummation of the great tribulation.

THE FIFTH TRUMPET announced the first Woe upon the earth (9:1–11). "And the fifth . . . sounded, and I [John] saw a star fall from heaven into the earth: and to him was given the key of the bottomless pit." The *Revised Version* gives the correct rendering of the tense of the verb as *fallen.* The *star* (here used symbolically as an intelligent creature with the attributes of personality) is seen by John as having already fallen from heaven. There is only one creature in Spiritual history that can be described as "fallen from heaven" and that one is identified as Lucifer, who upon being cast out of heaven became identified as Satan, the adversary, and "prince of the power of the air" (or aerial regions).

Jesus declared "I beheld Satan as lightning fall from heaven" (Luke 10:18). And now in the prophetic scene before us, having been cast out from the heavens to the earth, (Revelation 12:7–12) he is given (restricted) authority over the nether regions, namely, the keys of the bottomless pit (Greek *abyssos*), the abode of demons. Being given the key, he is also given permission to open the pit, "And he opened the bottomless pit; and there arose a smoke . . . as the smoke of a great furnace; and the sun and the air were darkened by reason of the smoke . . . and there came out of the smoke locusts upon the earth . . . ." The smoke darkened the sun with its density and out from the blackness came locusts. By the description of their appearance and activity it is evident that they were not the common locusts but appearing to John as a visual representation as locusts swarm over the earth. Coming from the pit, it can be safely assumed that these were demon insects, that is demons embodying these creatures and endowing them with power to strike "like unto the scorpions" inflicting painful torment until men will seek death and death shall flee from them (9:6).

That they are demon creatures is evident by the fact that their leader is Satan whose name in the Hebrew tongue is Abaddon and in the Greek tongue Apollyon—both names meaning *destroyer.*

The description that John gives of these swarming demon-creatures is almost beyond the power of imagination. For instance, he writes that they are like horses—not necessarily shaped as horses, but like horses in their preparation for battle. The crowns upon their heads were not actual crowns of gold but *as it were.* So it is that John uses the vague *as it were, as, like unto,* (not actually so) throughout his description. The overall awesome picture is one of terrifying torment (9:3–11). Verses 4 and 5 reveal, however, that the scope of their demonic activity is limited. Not to attack the vegetation and only to hurt those who have not the "seal of God in their foreheads"; this evidently excludes from hurt the 144,000 sealed ones of chapter 7. They (the demonic creatures) are limited not to kill men but to torment them. Further, their activity will be limited to five months' duration.

since war, famine, death and martyrdom do not follow in the wake of Christ's returning. War shall be no more, and every man shall have plenty, *under his own vine and fig tree* when Christ returns. But not so in the wake of the rider of Revelation 6:1–2; war, famine and death follow in his wake. The crown he wears is (Greek) *stephanos,* not *diadema,* the crown of regal majesty and authority, as worn by Christ when He returns to rule and to reign.

Besides, in Revelation 19:12 Christ comes on a white horse at the end of the great tribulation, not at the beginning. The rider of chapter 6:2 carries as his weapon a bow (no arrows) for we read of *the Prince that shall come* (of Daniel's great vision) "by peace shall destroy many" (Daniel 8:25; 1 Thessalonians 5:3). This refers to a period of false, deceptive peace for, as said of the rider revealed in the breaking of the first seal "he went forth conquering and to conquer."

In the short space of three and a half years after his arrival on the world scene—that is, after his true identity is revealed—this rider subjects the whole world to his conquest of tyranny (Revelation 13:4–8) until he is overthrown and destroyed by the coming (upon a white horse) of the rightful King whose weapon is not a bow, but a sword (the breath of his lips) with which He slays the imposter and his armies (Revelation 19:11–16).

THE SECOND SEAL (6:4). "And there went out another horse that was red: and power was given to him that sat thereon to take peace from the earth, and that they should kill one another: and there was given unto him a great sword." To *him* was given, reveals the fact by the use of the pronoun *him,* that the rider was more than a symbol. He was a divinely appointed agent, a man of blood, to take peace from the earth; as it is a day of vengeance, they (the earth dwellers) should slay one another. The great sword given him is symbolic of power to sever all ties of restraint: national hostilities, international treaties violated without compunction, civil authorities unable to check the flood of violence, riots, class wars, race wars, universal antagonism which breeds bloodshed and genocide, "that they should kill one another."

THE THIRD SEAL (6:5–6). "And I beheld, and lo a black horse; and he that sat on him had a pair of balances in his hand. And I heard a voice . . . a measure of wheat for a penny, and three measures of barley for a penny; and see thou hurt not the oil and the wine." The black hand of famine, the aftermath of war, is revealed by prophetic proclamation, "A measure of wheat for a penny." The penny of those days was the denarius, the current day's wages of the worker, reminding us of the lamentation of the people of old, "our skin was black like an oven because of the terrible famine" (Lamentations 5:10). No small wonder that this period of judgment is called the Great Tribulation, for hunger is a living death.

THE FOURTH SEAL (6:8). "Behold a pale horse: and his name that sat upon him was Death, and Hell followed with him." Next a pale (sickly green colored) horse is revealed. The rider's name is Death, which inevitably follows war and famine. The first seal revealed a false peace, the second war, the third death. These agencies of judgment, upon authority from the throne, are widespread in effect, resulting in the death of one fourth of the earth's population. Hell (hades) follows death (like the scavenger animals that follow the killer) collecting the souls, that is the immaterial, never-dying part of man after death seizes the physical body. Hell and death are terms used here concerning the ungodly.

THE FIFTH SEAL (6:9–11). " . . . I saw . . . the souls of them that were slain for the word of God, and for the testimony which they held." With the opening of the fifth seal the souls of those slain for the testimony which they held during the tribulation period are revealed as "under the altar." Here the scene changes from the events predicted to take place on earth as recorded under the first, second, third and fourth seals. Now it shifts to a scene in heaven, to a number of martyrs, faithful witnesses who had been killed on earth for the cause of Christ's Kingdom.

The term *soul* is expressive of the real person; the body, which is visible, is the tabernacle or vehicle in which the *living soul* is housed, and through which man can express himself through the understandable senses. Upon being slain on earth, men's souls are received into heaven and are pictured here as "under the altar,"—that is—having been offered as a sacrifice. They are neither the Old Testament martyrs nor the martyrs of the Church Age, but are distinctly those martyred after the Rapture of the Church saints. They were slain for the Word of God and their testimony during the tribulation period, which is when men shall revile the Word and the name of God as in no other period of history. White robes given them confirms the fact that in God's own way and providence some will be saved; through the church body, the Lamb's bride will have been translated from the earthly scene.

CHART NO. 5

THE SIXTH SEAL (6:12–17). ". . . lo, there was a great earthquake; and the sun became black as sackcloth of hair, and the moon became as blood; and the stars of heaven fell unto the earth . . . ." The judgment of the sixth seal unleashes devastating fury upon the earth. John beheld six great catastrophes purposed to shake the very starry heavens and the whole earth.

As terrifying as it is, it is not the final judgment. The judgments (so far: conquest, war, famine, bloodshed and death) were executed by the Antichrist as an instrument of God's purpose, but with the opening of the sixth seal, the agents of execution are the unleashed powers of nature. God has unleashed His battalions—the elements, lightnings, thunders, hail, fire, flood and earthquake—many times before in judgment, hence, there is no valid reason to accept anything but the literal meaning of the catastrophes of the sixth seal. Speaking of God's battalions we are reminded of Jehovah's question of Job of old: "Hast thou entered into the treasures of the snow? or has thou seen the treasures of the hail, which I have reserved against the time of trouble, against the day of battle and war?" (Job 38:22–23).

Under the sixth seal there is (1) an earthquake, (2) the sun darkened as black as sackcloth, (3) the moon becoming (red) as blood, (4) a devastating shower of meteorites, (5) the parting of the heavens as a scroll and (6) every mountain and island is shaken out of place, striking terror to all that dwell upon the earth. Kings and bondmen, high and low, rich and poor cry to the mountains to fall upon them to hide them from the face of God and the consuming wrath of the Lamb, realizing in their terror that the end of the age is upon them. In answer to the disciples' question regarding the end time, Jesus predicted the signs foretelling this very judgment (Luke 21:25–26).

JUDGMENT RESTRAINED (7:1–3). The sequence in which the opening of the seven sealed book occurs is temporarily interrupted. God has a purpose to accomplish between the judgments of the sixth seal and the opening of the seventh. In the midst of the scene of terror and fear God remembers mercy and restrains the storm for a season before continuing with the severest judgment foretold in chapters 8 and 16.

God, remembering mercy in wrath, purposes to seal a certain number of *servants* that they might be spared the judgment yet to be poured out upon the Christ-rejecting world. The agents God uses in restraining judgment are angels. All the Scriptures both Old and New confirm the ministry of angels in the affairs of man. (A complete and visual study of Angelology was chosen for the second Panorama series because of its great importance as the background of the spiritual warfare in the believer's life: Panorama No. 2. The complete study of "Angelology.")

Four angels are commanded to hold back the four winds (symbols of judgment) while God accomplishes His purpose—the sealing of the 144,000 Jewish witnesses to Christ as their true Messiah. It would be time consuming to declare who these 144,000 were not, for it cannot be stated more clearly who they are. They are literal Israelites—12,000 from each of the twelve tribes—each tribe named as blood sons of Jacob.

Israel, particularly, will suffer under the heel of the Antichrist whom God will use to judge that nation. It will be a time of intense trial as spoken of by the Prophet Jeremiah, "Alas! for that day is great, so that none is like it; it is even the time of Jacob's trouble; but he shall be saved out of it" (Jeremiah 30:7).

The four angels hold back the fury of the elements while the fifth angel, from the east (literally *the sunrising*) bearing the seal of the living God, carries out his mission of sealing the 144,000. What the nature of the seal will be is not told us, but a seal guarantees ownership and preservation. They are to be kept from the hand of the destroyer while they accomplish their particular service for God. "After this," that is, after sealing the 144,000 of Israel for a particular ministry during the tribulation, John beheld "and, lo, a great multitude . . . of all nations, and kindreds, and people, and tongues, (evidently a great company of Gentiles) stood before the

tative of "the church of the firstborn, which are written in heaven," as in the old order twenty-four elders were appointed to represent the entire priesthood. The chief privilege of a priest is access to God. Since the veil of the Temple was rent, the New Testament priesthood has perpetual access to the throne of Grace, for as the Apostle Peter declared, "Ye are a chosen generation, a royal priesthood, an holy nation, a peculiar people; that ye should shew forth the praises of him who hath called you out of darkness into his marvellous light" (1 Peter 2:9).

"And out of the throne proceeded lightnings and thunderings and voices." As the seer beheld the dazzling beauty of the heavenly scene, he was soon to realize that the throne of Deity was a throne of Judgment. Lightnings and thunderings are the awesome symbols of divine judgment, as when at Sinai Israel heard the naked voice of God and were fear stricken (Exodus 20:18-19).

"And there were seven lamps of fire burning before the throne, which are the seven Spirits of God." These lamps of fire are identified as "the seven Spirits of God." Again the number seven speaks not of seven individual Spirits, but rather the completeness or fullness of the person, the works and attributes of the Holy Spirit. The throne of Deity here betokens vengeance upon the guilty, and the Spirit of God charged with the fulness of consuming fire.

THE FOUR LIVING CREATURES (4:6).

"And before the throne there was a sea of glass like unto crystal: and in the midst of the throne, and around about the throne, were four beasts [Greek text, *zoa*—living creatures] full of eyes before and behind."

John's attention is now directed to four living creatures in the midst and around about the throne. The first like a lion, the second like a calf, the third the face of a man, the fourth like a flying eagle. Some think that these are cherubim referred to in Ezekiel 10:14-20; others speculate that each having six wings identifies them with the seraphim of Isaiah (6:2-3). Still others compare them with the four major aspects in the person of Christ presented in the gospels as the lion by Matthew, the calf or ox, the faithful servant by Mark, the humanity of Jesus by Luke, and by John as the eagle, the Divine Son of God. If these symbols are interpreted as attributes of Christ in the exercise of divine government they would imply strength, patience, intelligence, and swiftness in judicial judgment.

These particular verses (6-8) in the revelation give us no explanation of their nature; it is unwise, therefore, to go beyond God's Word. That they are created beings and that their praise of God is ceaseless (day and night) is clear. When they ascribe to God's glory, honor, everlasting praise and thanksgiving (verse 9), the twenty-four elders rise and prostrate themselves before the throne and cast down their crowns in homage to Him alone who is worthy, worshipping Him as the great Creator—God of all things including the very earth upon which He is about to pour out divine judgment (4:4-11).

THE SEVEN SEALED BOOK.

"And I saw in the right hand of him that sat on the throne a book written within and on the backside, sealed with seven seals" (5:1). This book must not be confused with *the book of life* which is a register of the redeemed. The book (or scroll) that John beheld in the right hand of Him that sitteth upon the throne, evidently contains God's climactic future of human history—the revelation of unborn centuries —the course of successive events needful for the establishing, in righteousness, the coming Kingdom of Christ.

The scroll is sealed with seven seals, undoubtedly in a continuous line, and not until the scroll is unrolled is each seal broken and recorded. In chapter 6 we are informed of the nature of the successive judgments of God to be poured out upon the rebellious, with Christ rejecting dwellers of the earth.

The contents of the scroll are of tremendous importance for they reveal the future, from the breaking of the first seal to the breaking of the last and seventh seal when the angel sounding the seventh trumpet shall proclaim the Kingdom reign of Christ and on into the perfect and eternal state.

When the angel proclaimed, "Who is worthy to open the book, and to loose the seals thereof?" John wept openly when he realized there was no one in the vast assembly of men and angels in all the universe worthy to open the scroll until one of the elders consoled him with the good news; "Weep not: behold, the Lion of the tribe of Judah, the Root of David, hath prevailed to open the book, and to loose the seven seals thereof" (5:2-5).

THE WORTHINESS OF THE LAMB.

John's sobbing ceased when he was assured that the Lion of Judah, who, as the Root of David, had the crown rights to rule and to reign in the earth. (See the author's complete visual diagram on *the crown rights of Jesus* in Panorama No. 3 *The Second Coming of Christ*.)

Christ is described as the Lion yet He stands in the midst of the throne as a Lamb, as it had been slain. A slain Lamb would bear the wound prints, thus, John could not mistake His identity as the Saviour of the world, for he was near the cross when the Lamb laid down His life. But John now beholds Him standing, alive forevermore in His resurrection Glory—possessing fullness of power (seven horns) and fullness of omniscient wisdom (seven eyes). As the Lamb slain for our salvation, He alone is worthy to complete the work of redemption by reclaiming the dominion lost in Adam and usurped by Satan. Redemption goes far beyond the ruin as we behold God's purpose in the redeemed.

"And he came and took the book" (5:7-14). The supreme moment for which all creation groaned and all saints have longed, hoped and prayed for has come. In preparation for the coming inauguration of His Kingdom, the elders, the living ones and all in heaven prostrated themselves before the Lamb and sang a new song of Redemption's Glory, and thousands upon thousands of angels joined in the worship saying, "Worthy is the Lamb that was slain." For among their hosts were legions who witnessed His passion and were ready at the Father's bidding to deliver Him had He called (Matthew 26:53).

CHART NO. 4

THE BREAKING OF THE FIRST SEAL (6:1-2).

The opening of the first seal marks **the beginning of the great day of the wrath of God**—the terrible judgments to be poured out in the earth, the redeemed having been translated *ever to be with the Lord;* the church is nowhere pictured in the earthly scene. It is not mentioned until chapter 21:9, as "the bride, the Lamb's wife."

The Book of Matthew has been called the Book of Revelation in miniature. When the disciples asked Jesus, "When shall these things be? and what shall be the sign of thy coming, and the end of the world?" (Matthew 24). Jesus gave them a list of successive events which would mark the nearness of His coming and the end of the age. There is unmistakable similarity between these dramatic events marking the end, and the successive revelations contained in the seven seals, namely: war, famine, death, martyrdom, the sun and moon darkened, falling stars and coming judgment. The distinguishing features seemingly, run parallel to the events written prophetically in the scroll in the hands of the Lion-Lamb as He breaks the seals and reveals the progressive order of the judgments.

Chapter 6 through 19 embodies the judgment period of the great tribulation spoken of by Jesus in Matthew 24:21. According to the revelation this divinely predicted time of terror shall be executed in a series of three judgments: (1) the Judgments of the Seals, (2) The Trumpets, (3) The Bowls of God's Wrath.

There is a question in the minds of some that these are not three distinct and different judgments poured out in succession, but rather one overall period of judgment with the trumpets and the bowls retracing their part in the action to emphasize the intensity of the one whole contemporaneous execution of the judgment.

A vast number of expositors, however, with careful and prayerful study of line upon line, conclude that the three judgments—the seals, the trumpets and the bowls—run successively. All of the acts described under the seven seals are seven acts of judgment. The breaking of the seven seals is an act of the Lamb. Angels are connected with the trumpet judgments. God pours out the vials of His wrath. Until now God's throne has been the throne of Grace, it is now the throne of Judgment.

THE FOUR HORSEMEN OF THE APOCALYPSE

The four horsemen are presented as symbols; (personifications not personalities) symbols of the human agencies divinely employed to execute the judgments upon the earth. THE OPENING OF THE FIRST SEAL (6:2) reveals a white horse and rider. Some announce that the rider is Christ, as Christ is seen on a white horse in chapter 19:11. But the only similarity is the horse not the rider,

THE MESSAGE TO LAODICEA (3:14–22).

The name of Laodicea means *the judgment* or *rule* or *will of the people.*

It is noticably significant that in each of the letters our Lord addresses Himself to the particular need or spiritual condition of the assembly; thus, in this, the last of the seven churches, Christ addresses Himself as the *Amen.* As confirming every word that He has spoken as the final, unalterable authority, the *Amen* is the eternal *So be it.*

Finding nothing to approve in the self-satisfaction and accumulated wealth of the assembly, our Lord immediately reveals His utter disappointment and nausea at the half-hearted, lukewarm attitude regarding spiritual vitality and life.

"So then because thou art lukewarm, and neither cold nor hot, I will spue you out of my mouth" (3:16).

They were neither frozen nor fanatical, but the Lord expressed the wish that they be one thing or the other—anything but lukewarm. Half-heartedness is the most difficult obstacle in the spiritual life of any assembly.

The root of their distraction from spiritual vitality was their smug self-satisfaction. "Because thou sayest, I am rich, and increased with goods, and have need of nothing."

So it was in the church, their boast was in their self-sufficiency. Absorbed in their material riches they were blind to their real condition of spiritual poverty—" . . . and knowest not." They were absolutely oblivious of the fact that with all their temporal riches, in the sight of the One who was rich and became poor that we might become rich, they were wretched, miserable, poor, blind and naked—(not destitute of clothes but destitute of the abundant riches of His Grace).

Reminding them of their spiritual poverty Christ said, "I counsel thee to buy of me." "Buy of me" was Christ's counsel. But there are some things that all of the material wealth of this world cannot buy—"gold tried in the fire"—the imputed righteousness of Christ that will stand even the fiery tests and never depreciate in value. What Christ was really saying, in fact, was the invitation of Isaiah of old; "Ho, every one that thirsteth . . . come ye, buy . . . without money and without price."

Though it would seem that self-sufficiency—we "have need of nothing,"—excluded Christ from the church, His appeal was definitely directed to the individual members by the pronouns *I* and *Him.*

"Behold, I stand at the door, and knock; if any man hear my voice, and open the door, I will come in to him, and will sup with him, and he with me" (Revelation 3:20).

This prophetic scene is one of the most pathetic pictures in the life of Christ, standing outside of the door knocking for admittance into His own church. Yet it is a wonderful lesson of Christ's patient love and His respect for the will of man. He will never force an entrance into any heart—He must be invited in; the latch of the door of man's will is on the inside. Then He will come in and share a banquet table prepared before the foundations of the earth.

Never was the material wealth of ecumenical Christendom greater than today—never greater modern structures, more ecclesiastical machinery, more worldly trappings of entertainment and compromise. Surely it seems, one can hear the boast of the Laodiceans, we "have need of nothing." But were it possible to ask thousands of nominal Christians one simple question, "Have you been born again?" the answer might well be as disappointing now to our Lord as it was to Him in Laodicea of old. We are reminded of Christ's own words " . . . when the [Lord] cometh, shall he find faith on the earth?" (Luke 18:8).

"THE CHURCH IN HEAVEN"

Chapter 4 begins the third important division of the book; **"The things which shall be hereafter."** While history characterizes the second division, "the things which are," prophecy is the distinct mark of the third division. Everything from chapter 4 to the end of the book is divinely predicted to be fulfilled after the church is taken from the earthly scene. "Things which shall be hereafter," is literally *after these things,* that is, after the course or consummation of the Church Age (chapters 2–3).

STUDY NO. 3

"THE THINGS WHICH

SHALL BE HEREAFTER"

CHART NO. 3

CHAPTERS 4:1–22:21

Chapters 4 and 5 form a prologue (introduction) and setting for the great sweep of prophetic events to follow in their order, as the panorama of future "things which shall be," unfolds before the rapt apostle's gaze. As he beheld, he saw "a door . . . opened in heaven," and John finds himself in the immediate presence of the One upon the Throne.

The first voice that he hears is as the voice of a trumpet (as in chapter 1:10). The voice invited John to "Come up hither." The words remind us of the experience anticipated by the church at the time of the Rapture. Although the scene does not actually formulate the doctrine of the translation per se, it seems to represent the order of the two great events —first the termination of the church's earthly pilgrimage at the Rapture, then the church in Heaven. As Walter Scott writes, the history of the church has been written, the overcomers have been translated to meet the Lord in the air, the great guilty company of mere Christian professors have been *spued out.*—Now, in chapter 4 the glorified saints are seen in heaven in the very presence of God. To be there, as seen in the prophetic vision, they must have necessarily been translated—*caught up*—thus, fulfilling the divine promise as revealed in 1 Thessalonians 4:14–18.

The word *church* does not occur again in the revelation until 22:16. Being "*delivered* . . . from the wrath to come" (1 Thessalonians 1:10), she has no part in the terrible scenes of the Great Tribulation and the outpouring of the judgments of God which form the remaining chapters of the book.

THE THRONE OF THE ETERNAL.

" . . . And, behold, a throne was set in heaven, and one sat on the throne." The central subject John beheld in the heavenly scene was a throne, with One sitting upon it. The first impression was of dazzling beauty and color—like a jasper and a sardine stone of deep red hue, perhaps bespeaking of the purity and the redemptive purpose of the Godhead, for as Seiss in his fine book *The Apocalypse* declares, "Here is the unnameable, indescribable Godhead, in which Father, Son, and Holy Ghost are consubstantial and co-eternal." A rainbow like unto an emerald, enhancing the beauty, in an unbroken circle "around about the throne," a covenant to the eternal ages that "his mercy endureth forever."

THE ROYAL REDEEMED.

"And around about the throne, were four and twenty seats: (Greek *thronos*—*throne*) and upon the seats I saw four and twenty elders sitting, clothed in white raiment; and they had on their heads crowns of gold" (4:4).

There is some diversity of opinion as to who these twenty-four actually are. Verses 10 and 11 seem to identify them as both a royal and priestly company of the redeemed. Wearing the golden crowns (Greek *stephanos*—*the crown of a victor,* not *diadema*—*the crown of sovereign authority*) upon their heads and being seated on thrones denote their royal prerogative. Their white raiment confirms the divine appointment, "Unto him that loved us, and washed us from our sins in his own blood, and hath made us kings and priests unto God and his Father" (Revelation 1:5–6).

Some have thought the four and twenty to be celestial beings, but angels are not spoken of as receiving crowns, neither can they sing the song of the Redeemed. Therefore there can be little doubt that the twenty-four elders around the throne are represen-

resurrection; "because I live, ye shall live also" (John 14:19).

"He that overcometh shall not be hurt of the second death," is the promise to the faithful. When the believer dies there is no second death but life eternal.

THE MESSAGE TO PERGAMOS (2:12-17).

Pergamos has two meanings, suggestive of compromise. Its suggested meanings are *marriage* and *elevation*—a mixed marriage. The state of compromise began with the dubious conversion of the Roman Emperor Constantine who declared himself a Christian, and Christianity, once outlawed and condemned as heresy against the state, now was declared the state religion. By his edict and example it was no longer unpopular or perilous to become a Christian. As his power grew, he favored Christianity more openly—elevating the clergy to positions of legal and civil honors and authority. Thus, by his aid and favor, persecution ceased and Christianity became a state as well as a church. Compromise was inevitable until it became difficult to distinguish between the church and the world. History is the record of increasing corruption of the church, a departure from true biblical doctrine by attempting to combine Christian worship and pagan rites and setting the stage for the dark days ahead referred to in church history as The Dark Ages.

Pergamos was a center of paganism, as evidenced by the many temples erected in honor of numerous gods. It is not surprising that our Lord should say, "I know . . . where thou dwellest, even where Satan's seat [throne] is."

In spite of the commendations of faithfulness in the time of testing, Christ, He which hath the two edged sword (2:12), rebukes the church for compromise, and for some among them holding false doctrines displeasing and denounced by God. A foreshadowing of the gradual decline of spirituality and the increase of compromise culminating in the inevitable apostasy was divinely predicted for the last days. The message concluded with a call to repentance, a warning and a promise to the overcomer.

THE MESSAGE TO THYATIRA. (2:18-29).

Our Lord presents himself to this assembly as "the Son of God." The reason for thus emphasizing His deity was, perhaps, that in His foreknowledge the condition of the church at Thyatira was prophetic of that long dark period to be recorded in history as The Dark Ages. The rise of papal power failed to expunge the Book of Revelation from the Bible; it became a sealed Book. The era of torture, death and devilish darkness is now a horrible page in the annals of history.

In introducing Himself as "the Son of God" He would have successive generations know that He alone is the supreme and final authority. "Who hath his eyes like unto a flame of fire" is again used (1: 14-15) to denote the searching, penetrating power of omniscience—and "his feet are like fine brass" the symbol of Judgment (verse 18).

The church is commended for its works, charity, service, faith, and patience (verse 19). With these commendable qualities could there be room for condemnation? The penetrating eyes as a flame of fire saw much, even in the abundance of good works, to condemn ". . . because thou sufferest [tolerate] that woman Jezebel, which calleth herself a prophetess, to teach and to seduce my servants to commit fornication, and to eat things sacrificed unto idols" (2:20). Ephesus was lacking in love but had no tolerance for evil—Thyatira exercised love but tolerated evil—a paradoxical characteristic of human effort in the spiritual realm.

The church of Thyatira is rebuked for tolerating the false teaching of a self-appointed prophetess who openly advocated apostasy. In verses 20 to 23 the church is indicted for spiritual wickedness. Whether the woman's name was actually Jezebel is of no importance, the name is associated with gross evil and debasing immorality. Her unenviable record can be read in 1 Kings 21. To the godly remnant, those who resist her evil influence, Christ gives a special word of comfort and exhorts them to "hold fast" to the blessedness which they already have and await His returning (verse 24).

THE MESSAGE TO SARDIS (3:1-6).

The word Sardis, in reference to the church, means *escaping ones*—those who come out. Though the church at Sardis was considered to be a spiritual church from external observations, in the sight of the One which "hath the seven Spirits of God" (indicative of the fullness and completeness of the divine attributes of the One Holy Spirit) and "the seven stars" (the angels or ministers of the seven churches), it was actually spiritually dead, merely living on its name and reputation.

In the midst of its spiritual death and deception, there were a few who had kept themselves unspotted from the world. There is no commendation in the message to this church, only the recognition of a few accounted worthy (verse 4).

From our vantage point, between the cross and the crown, there are some scenes in the great panorama of revelation that are yet in the future, "things which shall be hereafter," that is, after the True Church (as against professing Christendom) has finished its earthly pilgrimage and is *caught up* ever to be with the Lord (1 Thessalonians 4:17). In reviewing the sweep of church history from John's day to our own, as a prophetic survey, the fulfillment is too accurately described to be merely coincidental. It is seen particularly, for instance, in the name of the church at Sardis which means *escaping ones* or *those who come out*, the worthy (spiritually alive) ones in the midst of a spiritually dead church. This description is seen to culminate in the history of Christendom now known as **the great Reformation.**

A remnant of true believers dared to *come out* to preserve and propagate "the faith which was once delivered unto the saints" (Jude 3). The Reformation of the sixteenth century was, next to the Apostolic Age, the most vital part of the history of the church.

"They shall walk with me in white" is the promise to the worthy ones. White, in the language of heaven, implies purity. These had escaped contamination and spiritual death to walk with the Lord in the purity of His Holiness.

THE MESSAGE TO PHILADELPHIA (3:7-13).

The name Philadelphia means *brotherly love*. In the survey of the spiritual standing of the assemblies before the Lord, it is refreshing to find a church which is faithful to Christ and to His word. The message to the assembly is one of praise. Christ declared, "Behold, I have set before thee an open door, and no man can shut it." The continued testimony of the Philadelphia church was made possible, or divinely ordained, by Christ keeping open the door of opportunity against any attempt by opposing forces to close it, and the assembly's faithfulness in its continued testimony.

This assurance of the open door may be prophetic of the era of worldwide evangelism and great missionary movements that followed through the centuries after the break with Romanism, when a remnant escaped the darkness of ecclesiastical corruption and fear to carry once again the light of truth.

"Because thou hast kept the word of my patience, I also will keep thee from the hour of temptation [trial]," is Christ's promise to the faithful lightbearers during the present dispensation of His longsuffering patience between the cross and the crown. That the promise is far more universal than the district of Philadelphia in its application is very evident by the words "upon all the world" and "them that dwell upon the earth," although, undoubtedly, the promise was given to the local church in the face, perhaps, of some impending persecution. This, Christ warned would be characteristic of the Christian experience; "In the world ye shall have tribulation: but . . . I have overcome the world" (John 16:33). The promise before us (3:10), however, evidently does not refer to the Christian walk, but to a particular hour or time of trial which will be world-wide. Referring, undoubtedly to Christ's own revelation concerning the last days; "For then shall be great tribulation, such as was not since the beginning of the world to this time, no, nor ever shall be" (Matthew 24:21).

In the promise to the faithful (Revelation 3:10) the Spirit of God alone could have guided John to use the exact language in keeping with the meaning of the blessed hope of the entire context. He uses the verb *tereso* (will keep), and the preposition *ek* (out of), and *tes horas* (the hour); that is, "**out of**" the specific period of the trial or tribulation alluded to. Although the great tribulation is unescapably the outpouring of the wrath, enmity and hate of Satan against Israel, and subsequently upon all who refuse to submit to his blasphemous claims, it is permissive only as God uses him and his unholy dupes as instruments to execute His judgments.

Therefore it is evident that as these great tribulation judgments are to fall upon the whole world, the only way of escape is to be taken out of the world. And that is exactly the way of God's fulfillment of His promise to those who faithfully keep the patience of His word; "I will come again, and receive you unto myself." The only exhortation in the message is to *hold fast.*

"He had in his right hand seven stars." The mystery of the seven stars and the seven candlesticks is explained in verse 20. The seven stars are the seven angels (messengers) of the seven churches; the seven candlesticks are the seven churches.

"Out of his mouth went a sharp twoedged sword"—representing divine Judgment—" . . . piercing even to the dividing asunder of soul and spirit . . . and is a discerner of the thoughts and intents of the heart" (Hebrews 4:12). "For the Father . . . hath committed all judgment unto the Son" (John 5:22), and the house of the Lord is first to be threatened with judgment unless it repent (Revelation 2:16; 1 Peter 4:17).

"And when I saw him, I fell at his feet as dead" (1:17). John, who during Christ's earthly life had laid his head upon the Saviour's bosom as the beloved disciple, now prostrates himself as one dead in the awesome presence of the glorified Christ, in His unveiled majesty and the consuming fire of His absolute holiness.

The Apostle is then commanded, **"Write the things which thou has seen, the things which are, and the things which shall be hereafter"** (verse: 19).

THE DIVINE OUTLINE OF THE BOOK.

Verse 1:19 gives us the key to the interpretation of the book. In this verse there is consistency in the division of its entire contents: **past, present and a future.** "The things which thou has seen" refer to the vision of the glorified Lord (chapter 1). "The things which are," have to do with the letters to the seven churches. They depict the spiritual condition which did exist in the churches to whom the letters were addressed, and still exist in the church universal throughout the full course of ecclesiastical history, even to the cooling affection of the last days (chapters 2 and 3). "The things which shall be hereafter" (chapters 4 to 22); these things are future. Everything revealed in this great prophetic division of the book will be fulfilled after the church is taken out of the world (1 Thessalonians 4:16–18).

These are the three major divisions of the book, and each division is divinely revealed as complete in itself.

STUDY NO. 2

CHART NO. 2

"THE THINGS WHICH ARE"

CHAPTERS 2-3

THE SEVEN CHURCHES.

We now turn our attention to the seven churches (chapters 2 and 3) to whom John is commanded to write. First, we must note that each letter carried a message to the particular church to which it was addressed. Each letter to each church contained a searching appraisal of the spiritual standing of the assembly in the sight of the Lord and Judge. The message also had a direct personal application, for each letter concluded with words addressed to each individual in the assembly: "He that hath an ear, let him hear what the Spirit saith unto the churches," and "to him [the individual] that overcometh . . ." (Revelation 2:7).

Seven is the Scriptural number of completeness. Many Bible scholars see in the seven selected churches (for there were many other churches in Asia) the whole Christian body at all times and places. Christ Himself, reveals the explanation that the seven churches are presented as seven candlesticks (lampstands) holding forth the word of light. This simile is also true of each individual Christian: "Ye are the light of the world" (Matthew 5:14).

Christ is seen in the midst of the candlesticks (light holders) as Lord and Judge. This was, and is, His relation to the entire church universal (Greek *ekklesia* implies *called out ones*), thus implying the true universal body of Christ; those called out from every place and every generation during the historic period of time designated "the dispensation of the grace." He is still building, calling out, saving and perfecting this elect body.

The majority of expositors of the apocalypse are, seemingly, agreed that it cannot be merely coincidental that the letters to the seven churches have marked characteristics of the professing church as it runs its full course from the fire of Pentecost to the lukewarm indifference predicted for *the last days,* before the true church is *caught up* from the earthly scene. A panorama of conditions, commendations, condemnations, exhortations and assurances is in chart Study 2, with a survey of the successive phases of church history from Ephesus to Laodicea, from the early spiritual standing of the church to the state of apostasy "in the last days," of which the Lord and Judge declares "I will spue thee out of my mouth" (Revelation 3:16; 2 Timothy 3:15; 1 Timothy 4:1).

THE LETTERS TO THE CHURCHES.

The interesting course of study contained in chapters 2 and 3, suggesting a prophetic panorama of the professing church throughout the present dispensation, is without doubt the key to the understanding of this important division of the Revelation. The names of the churches are significant in their successive order. If the order of the names were changed they would not apply to that particular period of the church's history. This theory does not deny the local, congregational, and personal application of the letters' contents, but looking back in historic retrospect we cannot but realize that the messages did have a prophetic significance as viewed from John's day. This is the only division of the Apocalypse that has to do with the present.

EPHESUS MEANS "DESIRABLE."

A picture of the church as it was in the beginning, when the Lord held *the stars* (His ministers) in His right hand—the place of possession and authority. He was there "in the midst," to encourage, admonish, reprove, correct and guide. The church, then, walked in separation from the world. This is God's *desirable.* Ephesus was the center of heathen idolatry—the Christian assembly was "the lightholder" in the stronghold of Satan.

Ephesus is commended for its labor, patient endurance and spiritual discernment. The commendation, however, was followed by a strong note of reproof: "nevertheless I have somewhat against thee, because thou hast left thy first love." The exhortation was to repent and to do (repeat) her first works of love. Lest (without repentance) her candlestick be removed—an assembly but no longer a lampstand.

The promise "to him that overcometh," by which each letter is concluded, although the message is addressed to the assembly through its messenger (as the word *angel* implies), there is an appeal to the individual Christian to respond to the admonition and warning. The promise for overcomers is not for a special group addressed in each assembly who have been especially victorious, but rather to "He that hath an ear, let him hear what the Spirit saith . . . ." In 1 John 5: 5 the apostle asks, "Who is he that overcometh the world?" He answers his own question, "He that believeth that Jesus is the Son of God."

THE MESSAGE TO SMYRNA.

Smyrna means *myrrh* (actually *bitter*), a symbol of suffering. Myrrh had to be crushed to give out its fragrance. Fierce persecution had its center in Smyrna. The assembly was crushed under the stringent imperial laws against Christianity, yet the fragrance of their devotion triumphed above the two centuries of almost constant martyrdom. The persecution had begun in John's day but was prophetic of the cruel persecution of Christians during the successive reigns of the deified emperors of pagan Rome. The message commends them for their faithfulness in tribulation and poverty, and reminds them that in spite of their afflictions they are (spiritually) rich.

In the exhortation "be thou faithful unto death," they were comforted and assured that the words were spoken by the one "which was dead and is alive." Thus, assuring them of the triumph of His

STUDY NO. 1

"THE THINGS WHICH THOU HAST SEEN"

CHAPTER 1

CHART NO. 1

INTRODUCTION

"The Revelation of Jesus Christ, which God gave unto him, to shew unto his servants things which must shortly come to pass; and he [Jesus Christ] sent and signified it by his angel unto his servant John" (Revelation 1:1).

In the opening verse of the Book of Revelation we are introduced immediately to Jesus Christ, whose personal appearance is the subject, center, and purpose of the book—the capstone of all Scripture. Revelation is the book of consummation, gathering the threads of the Old and New Testaments and weaving them into one clear and complete tapestry of the divine purpose.

The true title of the book provides us with the key to understanding its simple truths and its mystical symbolisms. John, the recorder, was commanded not to seal the book, and a special blessing is promised to those who read and keep in mind and heart its precepts and admonitions, "for the time is at hand," indicating that its contents are meant to clarify not to mystify the reader.

The word *revelation* (Greek *apokalupsis*), from which our English word *apocalypse* is derived, conveys the idea of an appearing, an unveiling, a manifestation.

The opening verse introduces us immediately to the person and central theme of the book. It is the revelation, or apocalypse of Jesus Christ in His own person, unveiled from His present invisible estate to visible estate to mortal view, when "every eye shall see him." The glorious event which Paul refers to as the time " . . . when the Lord Jesus shall be revealed from heaven with his mighty angels, in flaming fire taking vengeance on them that know not God, and, that obey not the gospel of our Lord Jesus Christ: Who shall be punished with everlasting destruction from the presence of the Lord, and from the glory of his power; When he shall come to be glorified in his saints, and to be admired in all them that believe . . . in that day" (2 Thessalonians 1:7-10).

These three verses are a divine summary of the Book of Revelation of the Lord Jesus Christ. The substance of the book indicates not only Jesus Christ revealed, but **Christ revealing** the details of the divine mysteries, that is, truths which God had veiled until His appointed time of revelation.

In the words "which God gave unto him" (Christ) we see the divine order of communication: God the Father gave the revelation to Jesus Christ the Son: Christ employed an angel to communicate it to John: John was commanded to record it and give it to the churches.

While writing particularly to the seven churches in Asia (selected churches, for there were many more in Asia) which were representative assemblies both as to church history and spirituality, as to short comings and commendations; the object of the revelation is "to show unto his [Christ's] servants things which must shortly come to pass."

In the study of eschatology (the doctrine of last, or final things) which is declared as coming to pass *in the latter days* is here described as *shortly* (Greek *en tachei*), an adjective denoting swiftness. God is long suffering, but the end will surely come, and when *these things* (the divinely predicted series of judgments) begin to come to pass their execution will be carried out with sudden swiftness.

The Scriptures clearly teach, however, the comforting assurance that God's people will escape "the wrath to come" (1 Thessalonians 1:10; Revelation 3:10); as seen in the heavenly vision of a royal company of redeemed and glorified saints, crowned and seated around about the throne in heaven (Revelation 4:1-4).

THE VISION OF THE GLORIFIED CHRIST
(Revelations 1:9-20).

"I John, who also am your brother, and companion [fellow partaker] in tribulation . . . was in the isle that is called Patmos, for the word of God, and the testimony of Jesus Christ."

In verse 10 John delares "I was [became] in the Spirit." In the Greek text the article is omitted, reading, "I became in Spirit." This implies a state of spiritual ecstasy—his whole being taken full possession of by the Holy Spirit, thereby receptive to the revelation to follow. "On the Lord's day"—the Lord's day only occurs once in the Bible (Revelation 1:10), but as the adjective *kuriakos* is translated *the Lord's*, the appellation was used commonly as a purely Christian word, associated with the Christian's special day of rest and worship. "The first day of the week" was the resurrection day of our Lord (John 20:1-19).

The period of **coming judgment** is spoken of as "the day of the Lord," an expression employed to set forth the prophetic day of God's wrath. Thus, the vision of the glorified Christ in the midst of the churches (1:13), and His command to John to write to the churches "the things that thou hast seen," namely, the vision of the glorified Lord (1:9-18); "and the things which are," namely, the churches of John's day, representative of all assemblies, even to subsequent generations; *these things* most certainly have to do with the glorified Christ and His church, over which He "is the head" (Ephesians 5:23). Thus, the vision is of present application and could have no place or meaning in the future "day of the Lord" which is referred to as "the day of wrath and . . . judgment."

While in the state of spiritual ecstasy, the first thing that caused the seer to realize the tremendous import of what was to follow was "a great voice, as of a trumpet," commanding him to write what he saw in a book, and to "send it unto the seven churches which are in Asia." "What thou seest," suggests that the entire apocalyptic vision be communicated to each of the seven churches, with a special message to each individual church named in its geographical location, as recorded in detail in chapters 2 and 3.

Turning to see the voice that spoke with him John saw "seven golden candlesticks" (lampstands or light holders), and in their midst "one like unto the Son of man, clothed with a garment down to the foot, and girt about the paps with a golden girdle."

It has been suggested that Christ is presented here as a great High Priest of His people, represented by the seven churches here addressed. He is, indeed, a Priest, but a priest invested with royal prerogatives, in the midst of the lightbearers, as both Lord and Judge. This relationship cannot be limited to the seven local churches in Asia, but must embody believers, ("where two or three are gathered together in [His] name" Matthew 18:20) from the apostolic days to the end of the Church Age—the dispensation of grace.

The independence of each assembly is clearly indicated and the responsibility of each is clearly revealed—however, the unity of the church as one body is emphasized in the teachings of Paul. The church is not made up of particular periods or geographic locations; it is a living organism, a body, of which Christ is the Living Head.

In verses 14 to 16 John describes the majesty, dignity and deity of the glorified Lord in the language of similes, using the words *like* and *as*; the only way the seer could convey the glory to finite minds.

"His head and his hairs were white like wool, as white as snow," suggestive, not of age, but of the wisdom of the One who is from everlasting to everlasting, and of the purity of His holiness.

"His eyes were as a flame of fire." Piercing, searching judgment, "for there is nothing covered, . . . that shall not be known" (Matthew 10:26).

"His feet like unto fine brass, as if they burned in a furnace,"—they are like glowing brass, white heated in the fiery furnace. These feet that walk in holiness in the midst of the churches shall tread down all wicked abominations in the great day of Judgment.

"His voice as the sound of many waters"— . . . he thundereth with the voice of his excellency . . ." (Job 37:4). " . . . The voice of the Lord is powerful; the voice of the Lord is full of majesty" (Psalm 29).